THE

NARCISSIST

NEXT DOOR

by

WILLONA JEAN-PIERRE

DR. NES INTERNATIONAL CONSULTING & PUBLISHING

PASADENA, CA   LOS ANGELES, CA

Dr. Nes International Consulting & Publishing
P.O. Box 70167
Pasadena, CA 91117
www.drnesintl.com

Unless otherwise indicated, all scripture quotations are taken from The King James Version/Amplified Bible Parallel Edition Copyright 1995 by The Zondervan Corporation and the Lockman Foundation. All rights reserved.

The books recount certain events in the life of Willona Jean-Pierre according to her recollection and perspective. The purpose of this book is not to defame the character of any person or party, but to empower and motivate readers to face their truths despite challenges and obstacles.

ISBN: 978-1-949461-03-9

Senior Editor & Proofer: Dr. Danielle Clark
Cover Design: Jessica Land

DEDICATION

I dedicate this book to my bloodline. To my children Jasmine, Za'Vier, Dexter, Jordan, and Nicholas, that from you and every generation beyond will be blessed with healthy productive relationships and that every generational curse is broken.

All blank pages are intentional

TABLE OF CONTENTS

WILLONA JEAN-PIERRE

INTRODUCTION

He's handsome, charming, smart, motivated and so helpful to others. Everyone loves him and he's always there when you need him—much like the guy next door. People know him to be loving and hardworking—a man with good family values. Everyone thinks she's so lucky to have a guy like him. "You have such a good husband," many would often say. She's not too bad herself. She's pretty, caring, intelligent, and empathetic. She plays her role well, but it's not about her. She's a keeper—a trophy if you will—perfect for his image. They don't want to be the Jones' they are the Jones. They are young and educated. They have their own home, fancy cars, and treat themselves to lavish vacations regularly. They have what most people desire. They are the 'American Dream.' They are truly marriage goals. Only there's one problem—things are not always what they appear to be. The "image" that's being portrayed is skewed to the outsiders looking in. What's going on in that picture-perfect home is anything but perfect. There's a dark secret lurking beyond the white picket fence and behind that beautiful, stained, glass door. A secret that everyone who lives there is trained to keep.

Does this sound familiar? Are you in partnership with someone to keep a polished image but something entirely different is lurking behind closed doors? Does it seem like you're becoming emotionally drained with no relief in sight? Are your best efforts and cries for better days falling on deaf ears? Are you fighting a losing battle because your teammate seems to be fighting against you, and not with or for you? Nothing ever seems to get resolved. No matter how many discussions you and your partner have, they are on a constant tangent to prove you wrong and unworthy. In fact, it may even feel as if they are keeping score on your wrongdoings. You are in constant fight or flight mode.

I entered into a relationship as a tender nineteen-year-old girl. I didn't realize that the next fifteen years of my life would become a whirlwind setting of toxicity and abuse—but boy did I learn. I left that relationship with an abundance of knowledge through the first-hand experience on how to understand narcissism. I was married for a total of thirteen years before realizing I was in a dead-end marriage. A marriage that was going nowhere and was destroying my identity, my sense-of-self, the best parts of me. I don't believe that I went through this pain in vain. I had to go through these trials so that I could have a testimony—something to teach and help others.

In this book, I am going to show you how to identify the red flags in a relationship. My main desire for this book is to bring awareness to toxic relationships—in all its forms—and how you can survive. It is okay if you have missed those signs before. I missed them too. But this book will help you connect those dots, read those signs, and save your life. It will also help you to understand why certain relationships have become daunting for you. I am passionate about educating young men and women on how to avoid being lured into these lose-lose situations and wasting their precious time and lives. I have found my own freedom in pulling back the sheets of a narcissist's charade and uncovering truths behind what I have endured. You will find that same freedom after reading this book. I am living proof that you can escape the plot that was designed to destroy you. When doubt or uncertainty clouds your mind, and a toxic relationship keeps you in a gloom of confusion, there's a way out. This book will push back the clouds and expose the sun—shedding light on what has been hidden from plain sight. Get ready to be free! It is time to reclaim your life.

WILLONA JEAN-PIERRE

1

NARCISSIST NEXT DOOR

I was resting comfortably in my bed alone. I thought to myself, finally some peace and quiet despite all of the arguing and confusion that I've been through. Next thing I know my husband came home. He came into our room and took off his clothes, got into the shower, and climbed into the bed without saying a word. This all seems like normal behavior for a married couple, right? Wrong! My husband had been gone for months. In my mind we were separated. I think in his mind he could come home and go as he pleased. In fact, I believe he thought we were 'taking a break'. I'm not quite sure, however, in my mind you can't argue with your spouse for months, or even years at a time, leave, and then come back whenever you please and act like nothing ever happened. This can't happen, especially with no communication in between. I asked him, "What are you doing here?" He turned nonchalantly and answered, "I live here." I said to him, "No you don't, you left!" We went back and forth as we were known to do in these moments filled with tension. He then began to bring up what we were initially fighting for before he left. The conversation was old; we talked about it before, over and over again. In fact, I was tired of repeating the cycle and having no resolution or end to the problem. I was done! I was in that "when a woman's fed up" type of done. He hated that I did not want to listen anymore. He began to scold me about his needs and how I should know what to do without him having to tell me. I told him that's called mind reading and I'm incapable of doing that. The arrogance, sarcasm, and domineering attitude that exuded from his demeanor was a regular thing and I just could not take it anymore. I said something that I never thought I could say to him. I said something that I had never said before. I blurted out, "you need to quit acting like a Bitch and open your mouth and say what you want instead of expecting me to read your mind." Those words must have triggered something in him. We never spoke that way to each other. This was a first. There was a pause. An awkward silence that was tense enough to suffocate a room surrounded the atmosphere in such a way that everything felt still. At this moment, I could hear my heart beat and could feel the anger from his body form. I'm sure that statement left him in shock and in disbelief. This was never a way in which we communicated. It left me at an uncertainty to how he would react and what he would do. Although he has never physically laid a hand on me, I wasn't sure what he would do, and I didn't want to find out. Fear overwhelmed me. The anger in his eyes left me numb. He jumped on top of me and held my arms down. I stared screaming loudly, "Let me go!" My mom was in the room down the hall and I screamed for her presence. She had come to Texas to live with us from Chicago a few months before. My mother was unaware of our marital problems. I always refrained from telling family our issues. I always thought that it was none of their business and anything that needed to be handled, I could handle it alone. Well, at that moment, I couldn't handle anything, and I needed help. When she walked into the room, he let me go. I jumped up and started yelling, "Get out! You have to go!" My mother standing there confused and unaware said, "What is it, what is going on?!" He laid down on the bed placed his hands behind his head and crossed his feet very calmly and said, "I'm not going nowhere." I was hysterical. There was no way that I was going to sleep in the same bed with him another night. He finally provoked me and got a rise out of me. He loved stirring the pot until it boiled over then he would sit back and act like he didn't know why I was acting so irrational. I knew how I could get him out. I picked up the phone and called his mother. I told her what had just transpired and firmly expressed that if she didn't remove him from my home, I would call the police to escort him out. I did just that—called the police and waited for them to wipe that smirk off his smug face. When they arrived, they saw the commotion and asked him to leave to deescalate the situation. He was compliant in front of law enforcement— he got dressed and left with them. By that time, his mother and uncle had come to assist him leaving without any further commotion. As he walked out, he was yelling, but I didn't care. At that point, his anger was for show and had no place in my house. It fell on deaf ears. However, there was one sound that didn't fall on deaf ears. I could actually hear it clear as day and with so much enunciation. This sound not only pierced my ears, but it also pierced my heart. This sound that I heard, was the sound of my children tears. No matter how fed up I was with my husband, seeing the pain in their eyes completely shook my core. When he finally left, I couldn't calm myself down. I was balling. I remember my daughter trying to comfort me saying, "It's ok mom." But that wasn't true. Everything wasn't okay. My mind was spiraling, and I had a trip planned to Las Vegas the next day. How in the world was I going to enjoy a trip after this fiasco? I bet you're wondering what events led up to this breaking point. Well, that is a long story and trust me, this was not an isolated event. This exchange was simply the straw that broke the camel's back. In order to truly understand, let's start from the beginning.

2

IN THE BEGINNING

Once high school was done, I decided to take a year off. I wasn't prepared to go straight to college because I had two children—one that I had right after high school—and I wasn't sure what I wanted to do. A year had passed, and my mother suggested that I apply for a nursing program. I never really gave nursing much thought, but I considered my mother's suggestion, nonetheless. After taking the time to weigh my options, and consider my children, I heeded her advice and registered for nursing school.

As stereotypical or sexist as it may sound, nursing school is comprised of more women than men. This was no different at the school in which that I enrolled. Because of this, a man sighting (in nursing school) sparked an interest for of all the women. In a way, it became a sport—who can get his attention first and win the prize. Well, one day, a new student, from the day class, walked in. I noticed him instantaneously and I thought to myself, "damn, this brother is cute!" He had on white Nautica shorts, a shirt, and a fisherman hat.

During class, I was very attentive and participatory. I guess you can say I was a nerd or overachiever. The "Nautica Guy" sat in the very back of the class. I wanted to know what kind of person he was. Was he smart? Was he paying attention like me and eager to participate? The professor called on him to answer a question. As other students and I looked back awaiting his response, I saw him with his head down, sound asleep on his desk. My thoughts about him changed. My judgement creeped in and I thought, "oh no, one of those. A lazy bum that just sleeps through class." I wasn't interested in those types. I wanted someone who was smart and sharp as I thought I was. Someone who was ambitious and ready to tackle life by the horns. Nautica Guy woke up and asked the professor to repeat the question. When he did, to our surprise, Nautica Guy answered correctly, without hesitation, and then laid his head back down and went to sleep. He wasn't even paying attention. My interest had spiked again, and I was intrigued at his intelligence. This was a reoccurring behavior for him. He would come in, sit in the back, sleep, get called on, answer the questions correctly, and then go back to sleep. I later learned that Nautica Guy was working night shift as a CNA and was going to school during the day. He wasn't uneducated, he was just tired, and for some reason, that impressed me even more. I wanted to learn more about him. I was ashamed at my judgmental thoughts about him but also relieved that he wasn't what I thought he was. A few weeks had passed, and our class began to have clinicals. We were soon assigned what our respective hospitals for clinicals. There were 4 different schools as options. I was extremely nervous about this process. I didn't have a car, and if I got stuck with a hospital across town, I would have to on the bus at night by myself on the days that I have clinicals. I wasn't looking forward to that. To my relief, Nautica Guy and I were assigned to the same hospital, in the city. It was 2 bus rides away. That was good in my eyes. I went from not being totally sure of what I wanted to do after high school to now being in nursing school. Not to mention, I now get to work more closely with the Nautica Guy and get to know him better.

I felt pretty confident during clinicals. Being in an actual clinical setting, surrounded around patients instead of in the classroom, was exciting for me. I was the youngest in the class. I was sharp, eager, and an overachiever. I began to love nursing and the thought of helping people and making their lives better, intrigued me all the more. Nursing awakened something in me that I didn't know existed. I was very young and eager so when the instructor asked who wanted to go first in clinical on the test dummy, I volunteered. I also thought this was a chance to get noticed by Nautica Guy. I needed him to know that I was the true definition of "brains and beauty." After being in clinicals a while, we began friendly conversation. I was finally getting somewhere.

I lived in the inner city, didn't have a car and I didn't feel like I needed one. The public transportation in the city of Chicago was very reliable. You could literally get anywhere you wanted on a bus or train. I learned at an early age how to ride both. Because I never needed a car, I never learned how to drive one. Clinicals were over that evening and, as the majority of the class walked to the parking lot to get into their cars, I began walking towards the bus stop as I usually did. As I began crossing the street, I heard someone call my name. I turned around to see who it was and to my surprise, and delight, it was Nautica Guy. He asked if I needed a ride home. I told him where I was going and asked if it was out of his way. He said he lived the opposite direction. I outwardly and reluctantly told him it was kind of far and out of the way—obviously trying to be modest and show that I am both considerate and understanding. Deep down, I hoped he would still take me! He insisted it was no problem. That was the beginning of many rides home and the brink of a budding relationship. We began dating throughout nursing school but kept it private from our classmates. We managed to get to the end of the semester and through graduation without anyone knowing.

3

NICE TO MEET YOU

After graduation, I could not wait to start work and begin our new lives as nurses. Soon, we both obtained jobs in our field, and it was an exhilarating experience. Me being kind of fresh out of high school, the work environment was new to me. I never really worked much, except for a temporary telemarketing job out of high school. I was excited to learn and see what opportunities and experiences were in my near future. I was even more excited to start making my own money. Things were going well. Paul, well Nautica Guy to you, and I continued to date. In addition to his family, I'd began to meet his close friends that he'd grown up with. I had introduced him to my friends as well. Eventually I allowed Paul to meet my family—after he insisted. He and I both could tell that what we would be a long-term relationship and putting off meeting family was nonsense. Eventually, everyone met, and to my surprise, it went well. Paul laid the charm on thick! It was very hard for people not to like him. He had a way with people—a way with making people feel comfortable and light around him, almost as reassuring them that he could do no harm. He was extremely relatable. That was one of the qualities I'd most enjoyed about him.

Dating for us turned out not to be a long-term thing. As young as we were, we started talking about our future together and began planning it. I was only nineteen. That wasn't unusual. I was mature for my age. I had 2 children that thrusted me quickly into adulthood, so I felt that I was levelheaded enough to make adult decisions. We began talking about marriage. Thinking back, it didn't seem like a frightening conversation as some would assume. It was an ordinary conversation about planning our future. As a little girl and later a young woman, I had never thought of having a big, beautiful, barbie wedding. I'd never had dreams of marrying a prince charming like most little girls, and I definitely didn't think that I'd be starting a family at the tender age of nineteen. In fact, I'd never thought of it at all. I'd never sat down and really analyzed what I wanted. I never prayed about it or consulted God about it. I never knew what I wanted in a man, a husband, or even a male friend. I didn't grow up with a male role model to represent what a good man should resemble. Somehow, the moment that man walked in class in his Nautica attire, "what I wanted" became clear. During the course of dating Paul, it seemed that I instantly knew what I wanted. He was sweet, charming, giving, kind, and said all the right things. He made promises to take care of and love me. And little-by-little, he was making good on those promises. I was in a good place. I was being loved and cared for. I was, in turn, sweet and soft and kind. I was submissive to his needs, a listening ear to his worries, and a vessel for his heart. Love will make you that way. It will bring the best qualities out of you and make you want others to feel the same. On the night of Christmas 1999, Paul proposed. I was so elated. Although we talked about marriage, I had no clue he was planning on proposing so soon. Nevertheless, I was pleased that he did. It was one of the most exultant times of my life.

Paul and I decided to plan our wedding a year and a half out. We knew that we hadn't dated long, and we wanted to give each other time to know each other more. We wanted to be smart about it. I appreciated his patience. He wanted to make sure that everything that we did was for the good of our relationship. Slow and steady wins the race, right? So, we spent the next year and a half getting to know each other more, courting, and also planning a wedding. I cannot express enough the bliss I was in at this time of my life. I was in love, just finished school, started a new career and planning my wedding. I was elated and living on cloud nine, to say the least. This feeling only intensified the moment that Paul and I began to talk about setting a date for the wedding. A proposal was one thing, setting a date was another. This felt so surreal.

Things were a bit peculiar to me meeting Paul's family. Before us mutually planning for me to visit his home and have a sit down with his family we had a talk. Paul mentioned that he wanted to introduce his family to me first, without the kids, so that they could get to know me as an individual, and without any judgement. I know what you're thinking, that should have raised a red flag, right? Yes, I know, and it did. Something rose up inside of me, but I suppressed it. I trusted Paul and his reasoning. Plus, I loved him, and he never judged me for having young children. Heck, he loved my kids as if they were his own. Why would he be marrying me if he didn't? So, I trusted him. He assured me that it was best this way. He wanted to make sure that I presented my best self to my family, baggage not included. Besides, my charm and personality would win them over. Naturally, I agreed. The first meeting was a success. His family was pleasant and exceptionally welcoming and inviting towards me.

Time went on and the next step in this "family approval" process was steadily approaching. The introduction of my children to his family was going to be the moment that determined our future. I wasn't sure what he had told them prior; if he told them anything at all. To make things easier, we planned another dinner date for his family to meet the kids. Oddly enough, as the kids and I entered, it had occurred to me that Paul had, in fact, not told his family anything at all. Jaslyn was four-years-old and Zach was two-years-old I was proud that they were well mannered children. Paul's family welcomed us in and was excited to meet the kids. His mother said, "Hi Willona your brother and sister are so cute." Well into my 20's, I looked a good 15 years old. I really didn't know how to feel about that comment. I could've felt flattered that they thought I looked too young to have children, or I could've been offended at the fact that they would assume such a thing without asking. To be honest, I don't think I felt any way at all. I just corrected her by saying," No, these are my children," and I introduced them. I waited for a pause, a moment in silence, a negative response, something. I was used to the shocked responses I got when I told people I had two children, I looked considerably young for my age. Instead, Pauls' family didn't miss a beat and happily continued to welcome us into their home. By then, Paul's family knew me too well, and they liked me too much to change their opinion about me. Paul was right. I guess his plan for his parents' acceptance of me and the children worked. Maybe this was the best way to introduce my children into their lives. I was right to follow his lead. We shortly found out that Paul's sister was close to his age and was also newly engaged after dating her boyfriend for a short period of time. How ironic was that? A round table discussion began so that we could talk details about the wedding. I was always up for being around Paul's family. I always received warm and welcoming vibes.

We all sat in the dining room of Paul's home. In attendance were his parents, both of his sisters, my future brother-in-law (the sister's fiancé), and myself. There was also pencils and paper in case someone wanted to take notes. The idea of a double wedding was brought up. Paul's family had begun talking about it with excitement and high energy. I felt blindsided. I had a hunch that this planning had begun without me, before asking or considering what I wanted as a bride. I felt like the black sheep that had to be the bearer of bad news. I interrupted and said, "I don't think I want a double wedding." There was a pause. By the looks on everyone's faces, I felt like I stuck a pin into the biggest balloon of the birthday party. I continued, "I just feel like it should be my day." I asked Paul's sister if she felt the same way, but before she could answer, their father interjected, "the reasoning for our suggestion is due to the fact that majority of our family lives either out of the state, or out of the country. Having them come back for two separate weddings would be an inconvenience, and someone wouldn't have the presence that they desire because of it." Paul and his mother agreed. Trying not to piss anyone off, I thought quietly to myself, "who says that they have to get married around the same time, or year, as we do." As nice as I was and as much as I was fond of Paul's family, I couldn't hold back what I felt. I still insisted that my preference was not to take part in a double wedding and that it took away from the individuality of each person. To come up with a solution for family travel, the family decided that Paul's sister wedding would be the day after ours. As much as I was flattered of their acceptance of me and the eagerness to help us plan, I just thought that it was something my fiancé' and I should be planning, asking for help, and including everyone else in the process. But it wasn't just about what I thought anymore. There were others involved and I was gaining a whole new family that I would have to consider, so I welcomed the help—except the idea of a double wedding. By the end of the meeting, I didn't get a sense that anyone was upset or angry with my inability to cosign on the double wedding. However, not being on the same page as his family made me feel selfish for feeling this way. Was I? Maybe.

The day of the wedding was here. I laid there in silence. I always loved the still quiet of the early morning hours before everyone woke up, but more so on today. In all the excitement and hard work that went into planning this special day, I knew today was going to be chaotic. I held onto those few quiet moments for dear life before the day started. I entered into that church as young Willona and left, hand-in-hand, with rice being thrown all around me, and my husband. I felt a big smile rise across my face as I realized I am now a grown, married, woman. Even though I didn't quite know fully what it entailed or know what would lie ahead of me, the joy of being in this moment was all that I needed. Something in me knew that I had to be responsible with this new role of mine. I had read the Bible and knew that God took this union serious, so I did as well. We headed to the reception venue in style—our custom limo—as all of the family followed. We celebrated with a lavish good time. Food, music, dancing, and loving speeches accompanied this special occasion. One thing stood out to me that I remember closely—our first dance. As the host announced the first dance, we walked toward each other from far across the room, and met in the middle. But something felt off. I didn't feel the loving embrace that I expected to feel when a husband and wife first danced as husband and wife. I didn't get the butterflies. I wasn't overwhelmed with glee or even had the passion to look lovingly into his eyes as we danced the night away. In fact, I felt nothing at all. We did the motions and the two-step, but Paul seemed to be preoccupied. He was looking around as if wondering who was looking at him. He didn't seem connected to me in that moment as I thought he should've been. Because of his absentness, I couldn't feel the way a wife should feel on her wedding day. I wondered if anyone else had that thought or felt the way that I did, but I was praying that no one noticed. That thought seemed silly to me though, because at a moment like this naturally, all eyes are on you. I just discarded the thought. I figured that maybe his nerves got the best of him because he wasn't a good dancer. Maybe he was on edge about being the center of attention in front of such a big crowd. Yeah, that was it. Afterward we headed to Cancun for our honeymoon, and that is when I learned quickly that, his absentness on the dance floor was the prelude to his absentness in our marriage.

WILLONA JEAN-PIERRE

4

MASK OFF

Upon returning to the United States as newlyweds, it seemed the honeymoon phase faded pretty quickly. I never learned what it meant to be a wife. There were no classes on the subject or even talks from any older women in my family. I really didn't think too hard or much about it. I just figured that the basics would do—make sure to cook, clean, keep him satisfied, and be an attentive sweet wife to the best of my ability. That couldn't be too hard, right? As a newlywed couple, life started right away. I was new to the suburban life from the inner city. It was cleaner, quieter, and more suitable, in my opinion, for raising children. We both found secure jobs in our field as new nurses. I was living as a real-life adult. Living as a married woman, taking care of 2 children, and a husband with a full-time job myself. I took this role on with pride. I felt like I could do anything. Soon after the honeymoon, I started to feel tired. More tired than usual, I mean exhausted, wiped out tired. I was sleeping more than I ever had. It was safe to say I was hibernating. Ultimately, I found out that upon returning from Cancun, we brought back a little gift. I was pregnant with my third child. Despite my new found condition, I had to continue to work, take care of a home, and my new husband. It was becoming a lot of work, but I just continued to do what a good wife would. My husband and I worked as a tag team. I worked day shift, he worked night shift. Although we were working together to start, build, and maintain the lives we wanted, we were not really seeing each other as much as I would have liked to. This made it hard to build a solid foundation for our new relationship. I figured it would pay off in the long run. I soon realized that my children had to adapt to this change as well. Jaslyn was five and Zach had just made three a few months prior. I watched my daughter very closely around my then fiancé, now husband. My observation was not that she didn't like him but that she was just so close to me. Paul would come in from the night shift desperately needing to sleep. My leaving would not allow Jaslyn to let that happen. She literally stood at the balcony door screaming from the time I left to the time I returned home from my eight-hour shift. Paul had attempted to make her comfortable, to get her to eat, watch TV, anything to get her to stop crying. Paul even said there were a few occasions where neighbors would knock on the door inquiring why a child would be screaming all day, every day, nonstop. Paul exhausted all of his options on how to get Jaslyn to stop crying, being exhausted himself. He just decided to let her cry so that he could get some sleep. When I came home, I asked Jaslyn what was wrong. All she told me was "I want to go with you". What I gathered was that she just wanted to be with her mom and that she would just need to get used to Paul. I was confident that she would. Zach, on the other hand, took to Paul fine. He was cool, calm, and collected, and didn't cause much trouble. After coaxing, I encouraged Jaslyn to be nice and give Paul a chance. I think Jaslyn finally realized that I wasn't going to stop going to work and eventually calmed down as time went on. She, however, still kept her eye out for Paul. She was just not feeling him. I didn't understand why, but needless to say, sometimes kids have a sixth sense we're unaware of—and I'll just leave it at that.

Wedding bliss didn't last very long. I noticed that things started to change rather quickly. It went from being busy working for the sake of our family, to being cold and distant. On one hand I thought it was the shift couples go through after all the excitement of the wedding had died down, but on the other hand I knew it was something more than that. I just couldn't put my finger on what "it" was. Paul was definitely different. Not the same sweet compassionate guy I met at first. It was like the mask came off. First, bills became a hot topic. Of course, that is never a fun conversation. Actually, it was always an uncomfortable conversation, but we managed to work through it. In my mind, everything was going well for what I thought a marriage should be. Mind you, this is my first visual of married life, so my interpretation could be completely off. It was hard. We both worked, but I did all of the cooking, cleaning, helping kids with homework, and laundry. I ran the home as I thought I should. In comparison to bills and finance, housework was also something that was never discussed. I just took on the task and filled the role that I thought an obedient wife should. As the stereotype goes, the woman's place is in the kitchen, and in the bedroom. I tried to take care of both accordingly. The feeling of distance continued, but I wrote it off as work on both ends. I worked day shift. He worked night shift. Not the most ideal situation for us, but the 'show' of our lives had to continue. Our only time together was our days off. I was okay with this schedule until one night, we had a fight and he didn't come home. He had NEVER done that before, so I didn't know whether to be worried or upset. Soon, I would find out which emotion would dictate the next step. The phone rang. I didn't recognize the number, but I answered it anyway thinking he may be in trouble and needing help. Well he didn't need any help, but it was definitely trouble. There was a woman on the other line. I had found out my husband had been unfaithful.

Where did I go wrong? Why was this happening to me and why so soon into my marriage. I thought it would be years before marital problems would occur. I knew that I wanted to give him another chance. I didn't want to move back home, but most importantly, I didn't want anyone in my business. I was, and still am, a very private person. Only a few select people knew what was really going on. The most important thing to me was my faith. I'd read that God hates divorce. I didn't want to disappoint God, at least that is what I told myself. The reality is, I didn't want to fail at marriage. I wasn't ready to leave this relationship. So, I did what most women do in this situation. I gave him another chance. I wanted our family to work. I wanted it to work so badly. What I didn't realize, and what most women don't realize is that when you give him another chance, it's really giving someone another chance to mistreat you. It's giving him another chance to cheat better, lie better, hide things from you better, because now they know that they can get away with it. A man can only do to you what you allow. I allowed him to cheat, so he continued the behavior.

I was happy that I gave it another shot because things were looking up for us and we were happy again. We were finally enjoying each other as a couple. Despite our work schedule, we figured out a way to have time for each other. Dinner with family, date night, and move dates with the kiddos; we made it all work. What I prayed for had finally come together. Things were not perfect, but the effort was there on both parts. When I say not perfect, I am referring to things that I wasn't accustomed to like frequent visits form his friends and family. Paul is Haitian and his family is close-knit. I thought that the relationship that I had with my siblings characterized us as a close-knit family, but after meeting Paul's family, I was wrong. They are literally inseparable, and at this point, I felt like I was in a polygamous relationship—Paul, his family, and then me. In my home and in our community, we observed (or was raised) to identify certain cues. For instance, wearing out your welcome. That means, when you're at someone's home for an extended period of time, and you would just know, after a while, that it was time to leave and let people have their alone time without causing the host to be rude and asking you to leave. Generally, people want to be kind and don't want to ask you leave. It's just good ole' hospitality. They hope that you would get the hint, such as, "I'm tired" or "well I have to go to work in the morning". That was something that my family knew and understood. It was like an unspoken rule. I never saw anyone having to explain this. I assumed because it was my experience, that it was common knowledge. Well, let me tell you, that was NOT the case for Paul's family. Another thing that I noticed was that we kept receiving out of town guests. Now, Paul had a large family from coast to coast—New York, Florida, Haiti, and Canada. I always thought that was so cool because I had never even been to a family reunion and I longed for that type of relationship and experience. So, it's safe to say that I loved his family, the structure, and values they had on togetherness. It was fun and uplifting for me, like a family reunion every time we got together. The family reunion I never had. On the contrary, my personality type is that of an extroverted introvert. This means that, as much as I love being around people, I equally love my quiet time and alone time with my husband and kids. Yes, I consider myself to be a socialite. I have fun with people and can be the life of the party, but moments of peace are how I recharge, think, plan, pray, and put things into perspective. I was beginning to see Paul's family and friends ALL of the time with no breaks in between. That was interfering with my 'recharge' time. I didn't want to be selfish and just think about me. It had a lot to do with our cultural differences and backgrounds. Like I said, my understanding of the "it's something you just know" had a lot to do with how I was raised. His family ideologies were a part of his upbringing and a normal way of life for him. He couldn't see it any other way. It was like he had to have people around all the time. That sometimes made me weary. Why was he not satisfied with just being around me, or even me and the kids? Why did external people have to come around for me to see him smile? I understand that it was what he was used to and enjoyed, but I felt like I was bending and compromising a lot on this issue. Even though it had started to get to me after a while, I wanted to be understanding. I often took the low road. Besides, his family was so sweet and receptive to me. However, that didn't take away my feelings on the issue. In addition to that, I noticed that no one ever asked if the constant company, gatherings, and many guests bothered me. No one ever said, "Willona is all of this okay with you or is it too much?" NO ONE. EVER. I expected if not anyone else, my husband, would back me up and say, are you ok? Is this too much? Or hey, it's time for my wife and I to be alone. Nope, that never happened. Paul was always down for the family thing. And not the immediate family thing, but the everyone, extended, second and third cousins, god-father and brother-from-another-mother family thing. He always liked a lot of people around. ALL THE TIME. I didn't want to stop that or come in between those relationships that existed long before I came into the picture. But, at the same time, I wanted to build our marriage and immediate family on a solid foundation. I knew that in order to do that, there needed to be time set apart for only us. So instead of mentioning how I felt about Paul's family constant visitations, I took the approach of presenting to him that we needed to spend more time together alone. He began to say that I was nagging him, and that I just wanted him all to myself and not be around his friends and family anymore. He took me wanting to grow with him, as me wanting to change him. That wasn't the case at all. I just wanted time with my husband! I wanted to get to know him. I wanted him to get to know me. I wasn't getting that, and on top of that I was being crucified for bringing it up. Who ever thought that having a conversation about wanting to spend time with your husband and family would come down to being called a nag? I thought, "Damned if you do, damned if you don't."

WILLONA JEAN-PIERRE

5

MOVING ON

Despite the family situation—you know, the issue with them visiting sun-up-to-sun-down—other areas were working out, so I compromised. We never fought about money. He was building trust back again and we seemed to just have a new flow. We soon started to talk about buying a house. This was an exciting time for us because I always thought about owning a beautiful home. Having something to raise our children in, a white fence that surrounded the house, and a porch where my husband and I could sit and reminisce about our happy life. That is the life I wanted to build with my family. So, we called a realtor and began the search. We started looking in prominent areas near the suburb that we currently lived in and found a few that we liked. We were ready to seal the deal. During this process, my sister and brother-in-law, who had moved in right down stairs from us, began telling us about their brother who had moved to Texas with his family and were really enjoying it down there. They talked about how affordable the cost-of-living was and how the southern hospitality was unmatched. We started to research the market in the Dallas, Texas area online. We discovered that, not only do you get more home from your money, but that Dallas, Texas had many areas that were family orientated and great for raising children. We planned a trip to Dallas shortly after to see if we liked it. In comparison to the homes in Illinois, we definitely were getting more bang for our buck. There was no denying that the decreased cost of living would be a bonus for our growing family. We headed back to Chicago with a big decision to make. Not only would our lives change if we made a big move like that, we also had other family members to consider. This move didn't just impact me and my husband lives, it also impacted our young children that we would be uprooting to a foreign place, and our family members that we would be leaving behind. In hindsight, this could have been a good thing—the distance I mean. I wouldn't have to worry about the constant invasion of his family, where I was starting to feel like I needed visitation rights to see my own husband. We could finally grow together like a real married couple should. I had a lot of praying to do. I didn't want to make a big move like that without consulting God and knowing for sure that it was His will for my life. God for sure answered because I received confirmation after confirmation. We decided that this move would be best for us, so we did everything we needed to do to relocate. Paul and I decided that he would move first, without me, so that he could find a job and a place to stay. In the next couple of months, I came down, settled in and found a job. To our surprise, the move was the least exciting part of our new life. We were now about to welcome baby number four. We were excited about our new life, our new start. Despite all the newness, excitement, and busyness of everything, something still didn't feel "right" to me. I clearly remember having a conversation with a good friend of mine over the phone. I started crying and told her that I don't feel like myself. In fact, I clearly remember telling her that I felt like I was losing myself. I didn't recognize this person who's body I was in. Why was I saying this? Nothing in particular was going on. We weren't fighting, arguing, or anything that would be the cause to me feeling this way. I just started to feel alone in a room full of people. It was almost like I would have outer body experiences, where I would know I am here, but I didn't feel present anymore. I felt like the bubbly, fun, outgoing girl was slowly fading. It always seemed like I was trying to get back to that place of the "honeymoon phase". The place where I fell in love with my husband. It seemed like I was living in a relationship just to get back to that point. At this current state, the love was lackluster, and we felt more like roommates than husband and wife. I desperately wanted to feel that spark again. I wanted Nautica Guy to glide across the room again and pique my interest. I wanted to feel—something—anything. Then, I just felt, numb. Not much time to ponder on it though. Life was busy, and I needed to keep moving. Love would find its way back home—eventually, hopefully.

After a while we were finally able to purchase our first home, built from the ground up, and designed by us. We were moving into a brand-new subdivision. We were one of the first to move to the area, so we even got to pick the name of the street we lived on. Of the choices we were offered, it was perfect that we chose the last street in the neighborhood, Love Lane. I wanted that to be the foundation of our family. It was perfect. In the midst of things not going as well as I liked, regarding our marriage and family dynamic, this was a very exciting time for me. It gave me something to look forward to besides the unwanted stagnation of the relationship I so desperately worked on—alone. Designing our home was refreshing to the unexciting norm that I was experiencing in my marriage. Before moving into our new home, Paul had propositioned me with an idea. Paul wanted to know if his mom and sister could move in with us. The new home that we just finished building, and he was already sliding in his family. He said that it would just be for a year. When Paul approached me with this, my woman intuition led me to believe that this conversation had already been talked about, and I was not invited to that conversation. I was the last to be included in on an idea that had already been decided. I just felt like I was in the minority. To be brutally honest, I don't know if I was being selfish or not, and I didn't want to be, but I didn't want this either. 'Being married into the family,' took on a whole new meaning. I thought that, when I was being vetted by his family, me having children would be an issue. When that went well, I felt at ease and accepted. I wish I knew then, what I knew now—I should have vetted his family.

As I had been prone to do in the past, I didn't hide my feelings on this matter neither. I told Paul that I didn't want his family to move in with us. I wanted to enjoy our new home with our immediate family. For the first time in our marriage, I wanted to be his priority and I wanted us to just enjoy each other first. I told him that his family was welcomed over any time, but them moving in was not what I wanted—at all. He didn't seem upset in front of me, but I just felt an unspoken anger or disappointment from him and his family.

Moving into my new home was bliss. We waddled in our accomplishment of finally having a piece of the 'American Dream.' We had accomplished a huge goal of ours and was able to share it with family. His mom, sisters, best friend, and a few other friends we met along the way all had a place to make memories with us. I loved his mom and sister's company. I was glad to have loving people around that treated me like family and who we could mutually rely on. This sense of security was extremely important since we were new and didn't really know anyone in the area. Eventually, however, some of my old feelings began to resurface. Paul's mom and sister started coming over frequently and without calling. I didn't like that. Family or not, when you're in a relationship or furthermore a marriage, I expected everyone to have respect and boundaries. Again, his family is amazing, and I loved them—in doses. With his family, boundaries were nonexistent. They would show up unannounced—well unannounced to me—and not think anything of it. I didn't want to say anything that would jeopardize our good relationship, but I also didn't want to continue to reward bad behavior. My peace of mind was at stake and it was becoming more prevalent. I was becoming more frustrated, so I had to say something. There were many times that his mom and sister would come over and never knocked or rang the doorbell. I didn't like it at all. I started thinking on it and tried to rationalize their behavior. Maybe because they felt comfortable in our relationship, they thought that it was okay. I mean, obviously they do this to all of their family members, so maybe this was a sign that they truly thought of me as family. On the other hand, maybe it was a cultural thing, and I just didn't understand. I didn't want to react hastily, so I took some time to weigh all of my options. I decided to have a conversation with him about it and how it bothered me. I told him he needed to set boundaries with his family. He agreed, with no problem, but with an indifferent temperament. As time went on, Paul's family continued to be intrusive despite my attempt to settle it. I thought that if Paul would address it and have my back, it would be more effective. I was left feeling like an outsider in my own home. I was the intruder. I didn't feel like Paul had my back at all. In fact, I had an uneasy feeling that behind my back, he was presenting the situation as me having the issue and not him. My own husband was throwing me under the bus, and I could feel it the core of me. Often Paul would attempt to explain the culture to me. In doing this, he would always compare blacks to Haitian people, making sure that I knew that blacks were lazy and inferior to his supreme people and that his cultural way was the "right" way and that's why Haitians were more successful than blacks. I was confused because, didn't he know he was black? It started to feel like everyone wanted me to conform to their way of living and not taking the time to acknowledge my feelings about the matter. I wasn't going to conform to this. I wasn't used to it. I shouldn't have to share all of my husband and be left with nothing. I wanted our marriage to work, and to get along with his family, but I wanted this with boundaries.

We were enjoying our home—well I was. It seemed like Paul had grown a bit colder and distant toward me. This wouldn't be the first time. During the beginning of our marriage he illustrated this same behavior, and infidelity followed. But we had moved past that. We survived that dark time in our marriage. However, I couldn't help but wonder is something was going on. It seemed that he focused more on everyone else but me. I wondered what happened to that sweet, charming, loving person that adored me so much in the beginning. The man that gave me a ride home after class so that I didn't have to take the bus at night. Where was he? Despite me vocalizing my contempt for the frequent unsolicited visits without notice, they continued. It was like I had to address it EVERY time it happened. The visitors continued, and so did my discontent. No one told me marriage would be like this.

6

HELLO NEIGHBOR

About 3 years passed of us living in our dream home. I felt accomplished as a young woman, especially my background. Things were going well, not considering the occasional couple spats here and there. I didn't know that there was more to come. Paul's brother was in town and during the visit I didn't know that he was at our house. I saw them outside, coming from around the backyard. They were talking, having brotherly time, and simply enjoying each other's company. Something in my gut, however, felt like something was being held from me. I couldn't quite put my finger on it, but have you ever walked into a room, and everyone stops talking? Ok. Yea, that is what happened to me. I blew it off because I was trying to learn that Paul is privy to his own life and that I don't need to be "in the know" of everything little detail. Him and his brother can have their secrets, I didn't need to know everything. Paul sat me down a few days later and announced to me that his parents were interested in purchasing the house next door to us. I did not like the idea of that. From the beginning, I appreciated the close-knit relationship that Paul had with his family, and I was just as excited to be a part of it. However, I felt like being next door neighbors was a little bit TOO close-knit. I didn't see how this would be beneficial to us. I definitely wouldn't be able to keep them away from the house, or even worse, Paul would be here with us even less. This was just too close for comfort. I inquired about their motive to moving next door. He didn't give a real answer, but I was extremely bothered by the idea. I understood that no one was perfect, no family is without flaws. I'm sure that I did things that people probably weren't fond of and that they perceived my own family as dysfunctional. The difference was that I wasn't attempting to throw them off onto anyone. I wasn't attempting to persuade anyone to change their thought patterns to line up with mine. Though I loved some things about Paul's family and didn't like other things, I wanted to accept the good with the bad, if you will. But with that, I knew moving next door was overstepping boundaries and impeding on our privacy. I asked Paul, "Why in the world would they want to move into the house next to us, where they could have any house in Texas?" Again, he didn't have answers. Truly I don't think he cared to provide any. His only concern was to convince me to be in consensus with what was already going to take place. Something in me started to understand that in dealing with Paul and his family, things were already discussed and decided before the information ever got to me. I was never asked for my input. My voice didn't matter. The goal was to simply get me on board. Paul didn't have a problem doing that because he never came to me with a demanding demeanor. He was never controlling or dictated anything outwardly. He never gave me an ultimatum. When approaching me, he always came with a meek posture, showing a caring and modest side. He presented things as a proposition or a suggestion. Because of this, I was inclined to agree to the terms, if not initially, eventually. I started to understand the pattern in which this was happening, and I was always the only one not in agreement with the plan. Paul's family was always polite and respectful to me when I was around. It was more of an unspoken understanding. It was the way they made me feel about it, especially Paul. His outwardly sweet and modest tone in saying things had an inward "get with the program" connotation to it. While everyone was enthusiastic about something, I didn't share those same sentiments. My inquiries were always deemed as negativity. I was Paul's wife, the Negative Nancy, the one with the problem. I didn't care.

They never took my thoughts, feelings or opinions into consideration.

Despite my disapproval for Paul's parents moving next door, the decision had already been made and it was happening. It was a happy time for everyone—except me. I even tried to be excited and "get with the program," but I couldn't. I thought it was weird, presumptuous and tactless. So of course, the guests began to come in groves. From Haiti to Canada, Miami, New York and beyond. It wasn't that I didn't enjoy guests. It was more that the compromise was coming from only my side. I had gotten to know Paul's culture, his family, and the way they did things. My input or opinion wasn't considered. No one ever thought, "well maybe this is a bit much for her." No one ever asked, Willona, how did your family do things? Is this okay with you? It became the routine that it was expected of me. I had to have a talk with my husband. I sat him down and told him my feelings about the situation. I told him that I didn't feel like we were a team. I was gung-ho about building a foundation between the two of us, but I didn't feel like it was a marriage between us. I felt like I married his family and that I was an extension or accessory to the already decided family dynamic that he brought me into. I expressed that this was not what I signed up for. Again, I got an empty answer that didn't yield much promise or change. Just something to shut me up. I started to feel foggy. There was always something going on. Whether there were visitors in town, or arguments, or confusion, there was always a misunderstanding and people not getting along for some reason or another. It was strange to me though. This family never really argued like you would understand people to argue. There was always unexpressed disagreement. No one would ever verbally state their dislike for something or their discontent, although you could tell it was there. It seemed understood that you shouldn't disagree or go against the grain. Issues frequently got swept under the rug. I didn't come from a family of chatty Kathy's myself, so I'm not sure where I got the desire to communicate. Actually, that does make sense. My inability to communicate within my own family was the driving force for me to communicate within my marriage. I didn't want unresolved issues to hover over our heads like a dark cloud. I didn't want to go to bed angry and wake up with an uncertain feeling in my gut. I wanted to know what my husband was thinking, feeling, and his desires. In my marriage I always felt the need to address issues head on in order to resolve them. Despite seeing his family dance around and avoid issues and my family be totally ignorant of them, I wanted our immediate family to be different and tackle occurrences as swiftly as they came. I could not do this alone. In fact, I was failing at it, because Paul was more concerned with his birth family than his own. In short, he never left his parents in his heart and cleaved to his wife.

Family gatherings weren't always loathed. Going back to the original spunky, fun person I had always been, I loved them. Where ever I went I was the life of the party, in my family or any party at all. The problem for me came with the total disregard of whether I approved or not. Christmas' were always packed with food, fun, and family. I enjoyed every bit of it. I liked the idea of planning, getting the house cleaned, decorating, and preparing for guests. I enjoyed helping my mother-in-law cook. I enjoyed the music, dancing, and conversations. Unfortunately, when I wasn't feeling up to it, or feeling my best, I didn't have the choice of saying, "I don't feel like entertaining visitors right now." My boundaries were always being crossed. Guests were coming whether I liked it or not. You may be thinking that them having their own house should have made things better. Maybe I shouldn't be complaining anymore, right? Wrong! When Paul's family came into town, it was always an event. It was convenient for them for the two homes to be right next door. Naturally, when guests came into town, they wanted to visit Paul's house too. Sometimes guest would come without my knowledge. While his parents have the right to have guests whenever they please, so did I. So, when guests arrived, they would always make their way to my house because, of course, they couldn't come this long way without visiting Paul and seeing what he has made of himself. Completely understandable. However, that meant that I wasn't afforded the opportunity to get my home in order for guest. A simple phone call, email, or smoke signal would have been better than just dropping by. It got to a point when the people arrived, I wasn't welcoming at all. There was a time that my oldest son came into my room and woke me up on a Saturday morning. Our house was very big so a lot of times the kids didn't sleep in their own rooms but in the game room or our weight room. He said to me, "Mom, there's someone in my room, in my bed." I knew he had to be mistaken. I said, "What are you talking about?" and he repeated himself. I opened his bedroom door, peeked inside, and there it was—someone sleep, peacefully, in my sons' bed. I went downstairs to find Paul. He was casually sitting at the computer desk in the family room. "Who is that upstairs in Zach's room?" He responded calmly, "Oh, that's my friend Brandon and his girlfriend. They'll just be here for a little while." I was very upset. "Why didn't you tell me they were coming? Zach didn't know who was in his room! Furthermore, you know that I walk around my house in various conditions, so why wouldn't you tell me someone else was here?" He gave me a dismissive apology just for the sake of saying he did. "I'm sorry, I didn't think it would be a big deal. Besides, it's only for the night." Reluctantly accepting the sorry-not-sorry apology, I went into the kitchen to accommodate my unwanted guests. As always, I wanted to be a good host. I didn't want the friction between Paul and I to inadvertently pull the unknowing guest into it. Besides, the tone of the home is set by the wife. I was eager to make our visitors feel welcomed, despite the circumstances. I headed into the kitchen and cooked a huge breakfast for them and decided to be a warm welcoming host, instead of the angry, upset, bitch that I could have been. There were other times when he invited family members to LIVE with us, not just visit and I didn't find out about it until the day they arrived.

As years went by the "good little wife" stance that I tried to take had dwindled away. Every instance of unannounced company and disregard for my input had chipped away at it until it was nearly gone. After being around Paul's family and friends over the years, I noticed that I wasn't the only one that Paul took digs at. No matter who Paul interacted with, he tended to place blame on everyone else for whatever the reason. I've seen him do this to his mother, sister, friends, and definitely me. I watched how the others would respond. I watched to see if they would challenge and defend themselves or furthermore, make him take responsibility. It never happened. Paul's idea for provision was that he worked two jobs to provide for the home. While I was very appreciative of that, I worked full time as well and at one point held two jobs. Craig was Paul's best friend. Craig was always around. While I liked Craig a lot, I wanted Paul to initiate sometimes and tell Craig, "Hey, I'm just going to spend some time with my wife this weekend," without me having to say it. The time never came.

Instead, what was supposed to be date nights or family nights included Craig, per Paul's request.

As much as I wanted things to work out, feelings and thoughts of the truth started to swarm me, that it wasn't. I felt my true self changing. I also felt myself letting go. I think Paul felt these moments as well because when I felt like giving up, he would come and rescue our relationship like a knight in shining armor. He would shower me with gifts and attention. We would go out on a romantic date or have a night with just him and I. Those times came few-and-far in between. They didn't last long when they did. I again noticed this becoming a pattern. The good times became less and less, while the difficult times became more and more. Every time I asked something of Paul that I felt was valid, I was made to feel like I was nagging him. He would say things like, "Do you appreciate anything I do?" or "Do you think I'm a bad person?" So whatever issue I had, got detoured to me telling him how much I did appreciate him and that he's not a bad person. I ended up confused and wondered how we got there. It had gotten so bad between us that, at one point, we talked about separation and divorce. I was petrified at the thought of this. I didn't want to give up. I wanted to continue to work hard at it, although it seemed all the work was coming from me. I didn't want to throw in the towel so quickly. I wanted to be his peace, but I also needed him to be my husband again. I couldn't do this alone.

WILLONA JEAN-PIERRE

7

CYCLES: WASH, RINSE, SPIN REPEAT

We had been married for 8 years at this point and we continued with our ups and downs, trying to work things out. The distance at times gave me an inner feeling that I didn't like, an instinct. I confronted Paul about another situation where I found messages in his phone from a woman. He had no way out this time. It was undeniable and he didn't have enough time to think of a good excuse. He was caught, backed in a corner. I wondered how he would get out of this one. Would he finally own up to his faults and take responsibility for the wrong that he had done? The answer would be a loud, NO! Instead, Paul began to tell me how my daughter Jaslyn had been very disrespectful and that I need to train her on how to respect adults. In all the 8 years that we've been married, Paul has never not once mentioned that Jaslyn was disrespectful or pointed out that he had a problem with her attitude or behavior. So, I found it very puzzling that he was just now bringing this up. Of course, I knew that he was using it to detract from the issue at hand. I wasn't bending, so I redirected things back to the original topic. He ended up getting upset and storming out.

My life and marriage seemed to always be in a ball of confusion. I realized that this was not love. It didn't feel like love. Instead it left like I was being treated like a child. Then, it felt like a parent that didn't love their child very much. I, never before this marriage, imagined being a part of this much drama. Things were becoming clear to me as I observed the patterns of Paul and his family. While everything looked good from the outside, real matters were being swept under the rug, ignored or placed on the shelf. The endless confusion was the result of that. I had observed that Paul's blame placing on others, and not taking accountability, was not just a problem for me. It was a problem for those all around him. The biggest problem was that we were all accepting his verbal and emotional abuse because it was being masked with his sweet smile, soft tone and portrayal of eagerness to help others. And, while I would call him out on it, no one else would. No one would tell him that he was wrong in a matter. The more I saw this, the more I began to see that these behavior patterns were deeply rooted. No one held him accountable, but I did not know why. When I tried to speak up, he either attempted to flip things around on me(deflect) or totally distract me from the problem. I didn't know what to do but pray. I prayed, went to church, and even dragged him to church with me. Nothing was working.

Paul did not stop his relentless attack on Jaslyn. She was not the same 4-year-old little girl that screamed and cried when I left for work, but she wasn't bending either. Before all of deflection, Paul was very giving to the children. He would even express his love for the children and staked claim to them. In my eyes he did just that. He would go out and buy them gifts and shower them with materialistic things to illustrate our love for them. Of course, Jaslyn enjoyed the gifts but she wasn't totally won over. Especially after the attack sent against her. There is an act in the Haitian culture where, when children enter into the room of adults, the children have to give a kiss on the cheek as a form of respect. I even had to get used to this way of life because if you didn't kiss someone you were deemed disrespectful. We as Americans had to get used to this way. Jaslyn didn't always remember to do it and Paul made sure that everyone knew it. Things went from, "I love your children as my own," to "she is an archenemy that needs to go down." She became his scapegoat when he wanted to get his way. He became so focused on her that it seemed like an obsession of his. His whole conversations were always about, "Jaslyn is disrespectful, she doesn't speak, she doesn't act this way, or she doesn't act that way." He even got his family to join in. They even were treating her a little bit more harshly than the other kids. After going next door to visit, Jaslyn and Zach would come home and tell me things that would make them feel uncomfortable or that they deemed inappropriate. When I would address these things with Paul, he would get upset with the children for coming to tell me. I told him that I don't discourage my children from talking to me about anything if they feel like they were wronged. He said they were just trying to cause a rift with his family. I didn't see that as the case. I never made my children feel like they could not come to me, and I wasn't going to start now. The more they reported back to me, the more intense the pressure got. All of these issues were streamlined from Paul's seed of disapproval to his family. He even had my own family fooled. He would only do this to those that didn't know the circumstances that were taking place. They didn't even realize that Paul was setting the stage for how he wanted them to view her, which was the "bad guy," the rebellious child. To make sure that I wasn't allowing for disrespectful behavior or letting Jaslyn get by with anything, I had frequent talks with her and would observe her behavior as well. I was stern with her in the fact that, in my absence, she was to obey Paul and the adults in his family. I inquired about her specific issues with Paul. She was still young, so I don't think she could express it at the time, but for the most part she didn't have one. I started to obtain a keen focus on things as well. I noticed that every time Paul wasn't around, there wasn't as much confusion. He worked nights. So, he was either sleep, at work, or with his friends. In this time, the kids and I was with his family a lot. We did almost everything together. Most of the time, when he wasn't around, everyone got along fine. No one seemed to have a problem with Jaslyn at all. When he arrived on the scene, I noticed a shift. Tension entered the room, and when it did, Jaslyn was the focal point for his wrath, and the rest of the family followed suit. Let me just say, these occurrences would very seldom happen in front of me. Most of these accounts are from instances told to me by Jaslyn and Zach. I wasn't going to allow my children to be attacked. No one could specify exactly what she was doing wrong except the fact that she forgot to speak to Paul, sometimes. I don't count that against her because the rigidity that he brought with his presence was nerving and unpredictable. That would make an adult draw away, let alone a child. One time I overheard Paul telling our youngest son not to be like his older brother and sister. He was trying to pit them against each other. It was always drama and the bickering between us was constant. The environment for my children and myself became toxic.

Talk of separation and divorce would rear its ugly head from time to time. Paul took it as far as retrieving papers and presenting them to me 'Paul-like' fashion. He came to me with a distressed, compassionate attitude. His approach was that loving me is hurting him. He made it seem as if our arguments are tearing us apart, and he didn't want to end up like his parents. He did not want us to be that way. He took time and present a written plan on how we would divide our possessions between us. He said that the kids and I could have the house and he would move out. He wrote out a particular amount of money that he would give to help sustain the house for the kids and me. He made sure to let me know that he would just remove himself because he just could not get it right for me and he signed it, to avoid us involving the court. He felt that I didn't like his family, nor his culture, and since he couldn't do anything right, maybe we're just not right for each other. I had to correct him. It was not true that I did not like his family. I felt like he was trying to establish that untruth to get released him from holding himself accountable. Certainly, I did not want to get a divorce so, we agreed to work it out—again. I even suggested counseling, he refused. I was becoming exhausted with these cycles. Let me lay it out for you: Firstly, I would want to address an issue. Secondly, he would start these long, agonizing, drawn out, exhausting conversations to deflect from his responsibilities. Thirdly, he would suggest separation, or divorce, as a means of escape, and then there's the finale. The fourth step in this reoccurring occurring cycle is the one that, I believe, men universally use to shut women up. This step is the woman's soft spot, and to be honest, its cruel. The fourth step is him coming back and saying, "I love you; I want my family to work." How juvenile. Yet, I fell for it every time. But in my core, I'm a strong girl, and time would tell how much more of his bullshit I would be willing to take.

Once, I felt that strong woman come out, and I told him that I was done. I planned on taking the kids and moving somewhere far, far away from him. Paul was desperate and showed that he did not want to lose his family. He did everything he could to prove himself. All of his attention and focus shifted away from everything else for the first time, in a long time. We were his priority. He wanted to prove himself to me. He even went so far as to set up a counseling session. I agreed. That's something I had been wanting and thought our relationship could benefit tremendously from. We even included Jaslyn. I thought it would be great to get a non-bias perspective to guide us to solutions for our problems, as opposed to going to family. To my disappointment, the session did not go so well. The points that the therapists were attempting to get Paul to see, were not working. He became argumentative. The therapist was trying to get Paul to see where he was wrong in certain matters and how he can fix them to build trust back with me. We needed to reconcile. It was a valid solution. Paul said to the therapist, "So you're taking her side?" Childish! He took it as an attack instead of being vulnerable and receptive to the help our marriage so desperately needed. The therapist was the only person aiming to hold him accountable for his actions and correct them. It only made sense that he thought the therapist was taking my side. He thought that it was noble for him to tell the truth and that everyone should be grateful for it, but he didn't want to go any further to correct the act. Now, I know what you're thinking, and let me stop you mid-thought! The therapist was a man, not a woman, so the "sisters, before misters," mentality wasn't an issue. The therapist just had common sense—something I wish Paul had. Hell, Paul was the one who found and chose this therapist! The only relief that I was getting was knowing that, without a doubt, I was not crazy as Paul called me when I wanted to address issues. Paul was just a difficult person. Not just with me, but with anyone that disagrees with him. That wasn't the only therapist we went to. About a year later, our marriage found itself in another ditch. We went to another counselor that he chose—a woman this time. He could not understand why she was agreeing with me. The fact stood, she was not agreeing with me at all, she was simply trying to get him to get him to take ownership for his actions in the situation. He could not. He would not. He absolutely did not!

When the attempt at therapy didn't work, Paul resorted to slander. The fights continued, but it was sporadic. To free himself from the pressure, he started telling his friends and family that I was crazy. I first found out he was doing this through his sister. One day his sister

Veronica called me. She sounded really concerned over the phone. She spoke with a caring, yet worried tone, and I was in a rush to leave the house. She said "Hey Willona, are you okay?" I responded back, "Yeah, what's up?" She asked again, "Are you sure everything is fine with you?" Annoyed I responded, "Is something wrong?" She quickly responded, "No, I was calling to check on you." This was weird. She doesn't just call to 'check-in.' I started to think that maybe something was wrong with her. When we got off the phone, I thought that was really strange. Later that day, Paul's half-sister called me. This is the sister on their dads side that they found out about in their adult age. I had a closer relationship with her. We talked more often and could relate more. I counted it as the fact that she was not born into the culture and did not live by the set tradition and rules that they did. She grew up in the inner city like I did, with her mother's side of the family, that was American. She said, "Girl what's wrong with you?" I said, "Nothing what do you mean?" She went on to tell me that she had gotten an email from me saying that I am having a lot of problems and felt like I needed help, before I drove myself crazy. I said, "What? Girl, I ain't send you no damn email like that. That don't even sound like me." The more we talked, we both discovered that Paul had hacked into my email and sent that message out. Had his other sister Miranda not called me, I would have never known that he did that. His sister Veronica never did tell me why she called me that day. Go figure. God only knows who else he had sent this to. I could not understand why a husband would do such a thing to his wife. He was behaving in ways that were unfamiliar to me. When I went to check my email, it was gone. He erased it, so I had to change my password. When I asked him about it, he couldn't deny it. I told him that he needed to go to his family and tell them the truth—that he was the one that sent the email. This confirmed my feeling that he was talking about me to his family and friends, which he'd previously denied and said that I was paranoid and crazy.

With things not going well for such a long period of time, and me refusing to conform to Paul's tactics of manipulation, he tried the divorce tactic one more time. He didn't realize this would be one time too many. It was evident that I did not want to divorce. I did not want to break up my family and I certainly did not want to disappoint God, but I knew this was a way out of the cycle. In fact, I didn't want to be the one that initiated it. My thoughts were that, 'if I'm not the one to file maybe God won't blame me.' In one of many of our spats, Paul filed for divorce to place fear within me. I later learned the that was a tactic he frequently used to get me back "in line". It used to work. The devastation and hurt that I used to feel when he brought this up or presented me with papers in the past was just that, a thing of the past. I never threatened him with divorce in hard times. I was tired of the charades, the cycles, the fighting. I was ready for this shit to be over. The straw that broke the camel's back was during the course of us arguing and not speaking with each other, the kids reported to me that Paul had told my son "don't marry a black woman, marry a white woman." I was enraged at the fact that my son was not even old enough to talk about the birds and the bees. So, when Paul mentioned divorce, I accepted Paul's offer and was relieved that the opportunity presented itself again. I think it took Paul by surprise. He was expecting me to cry and make another heroic attempt to save us again. I didn't have it in me anymore. I was ready.

Paul packed up and left for "school," in Kansas, in our van. That's what he told me anyway. Because his words rarely lined up with his actions, I didn't trust or believe many things that he said. We never sat down to carefully plan this out together as a team. I honestly think that I stopped caring. Plus, I was looking forward to the peaceful times that would come in his absence. He left and ghosted us.

A couple of weeks had passed by and I called Paul to find out what he suggested I do about his part of the bills. His answer was "I don't know." What did he mean? Did he want me to come up with a solution on my own? Did he not have any concern of what his children would eat? I was confused. I continued to plead with Paul about money, explaining to him that the mortgage and all of the other bills still needed to be paid. The mortgage company was calling frequently to tell me that we were behind and that immediate action needed to be taken. He didn't seem very concerned. After a while, Paul returned home. It was evident that things were unstable in our relationship. We had a conversation in front of my mother about what we needed to do about the bills and how we should split things in order to separate. Paul didn't like how the conversation was going because I wasn't trying to fix us like I always had in the past. I was totally on board with the separation that he initiated. The attempt to threaten me with leaving me didn't work this time, or it finally did. When I asked where the money was, he was going to give me to pay his part of the bills, he started shouting and stated, "I ain't giving you nothing." My mom's eyes widened in shock, because she had never heard him speak like this before. She was used to the lowly, humble, sorrowful, heartbroken gentleman that he showed when he was attempting to manipulate. I was glad he showed his true colors in front of someone. He held to his word and did not give any money for the home or his children. Then he stormed out. We were officially separated, and I hadn't seen him in a while, until....

I was resting comfortably in my bed alone. I thought to myself, finally some peace and quiet despite all of the arguing and confusion that I've been through. Next thing I know my husband came home. He came into our room and took off his clothes, got into the shower, and climbed into the bed without saying a word. This all seems like normal behavior for a married couple, right? Wrong! My husband had been gone for months. In my mind we were separated. I think in his mind he could come home and go as he pleased. In fact, I believe he probably thought we were taking a break. I'm not quite sure, however, in my mind you can't argue with your spouse for months or even years at a time, leave, and then come back whenever you please and act like nothing ever happened. Especially with no communication in between. I asked him, "What are you doing here?" He turned nonchalantly and answered, "I live here." I said to him, "No you don't, you left!" We went back and forth as we were known to do in these moments filled with tension. He then began to bring up what we were initially fighting for before he left. The conversation was old; we talked about it before, over and over again. In fact, I was tired of repeating the cycle and having no resolution or end to the problem. I was done! I was in that "when a woman's fed up" type of done. He hated that I did not want to listen anymore. He began to scold me about his needs and how I should know what to do without him having to tell me. I told him that's called mind reading and I'm incapable of doing that. The arrogance, sarcasm, and domineering attitude that exuded from his demeanor was a regular thing and I just could not take it anymore.

Months went by and we, or should I say I, was falling deeper into debt. I wasn't aware of what he was doing anymore. I didn't know if he was working or going to school. I can't say that I cared anymore at that point. I needed him to financially support his home and children, which he outright refused. He wanted to punish me for not conforming to his way. He wanted me to struggle. When I spoke with him, I told him if you don't cooperate, we will have to talk about child support. He didn't show any emotion or regard for what I had to say. It seemed that he was striving to make me suffer for not going along with his games anymore. I tried talking to his mother about it. I told her that child support would be on the table if he didn't cooperate. I thought maybe she'd reason with him. No one could. I was extremely reluctant because I did not want to go through the paper work and red tape of involving the courts. Paul always made it seem that if we ever split, we could be cordial with one another. I believed him but would soon find out, that was another lie. He had gotten to the point where he wouldn't even speak to me about it. He was being awfully difficult. After months of trying to negotiate a plan to separate and being backed in the corner by bills and collection agencies alone, I was forced to go to the attorney general to file for child support. Before I made any move that I knew would affect us as a family, even in this hard time, I notified every one of my intentions. I was hoping this would be a wakeup call for Paul, and then I could avoid involving the courts. Let's be honest, we have enough Black men in the system. I didn't want to add him to the list. I told Paul that I applied and that we had an appointment to attend to talk about funds, he agreed. We headed to the appointment together. I could tell he was not happy about it, but he voluntarily signed the papers and we agreed on what we thought was a fair amount that he would give. In fact, it was the same amount that he wrote up months before.

The day of the preliminary hearing for the divorce came. We pulled up in two separate cars to the parking lot of the courthouse. I had asked my mother to come with me. She said she didn't think this was a serious enough reason for us to get a divorce and that maybe we should try to work it out. Truth be told, neither did I, but I had come to a point and realization that after thirteen years, things were not changing. Paul hesitated and showed remorse. He did not want to go through with things. Many times, in the past, he recanted after my effort to fix us, but this time, it was me, I wasn't budging.

We were living apart for a few months now. Paul was living next door with his parents. I heard of talk that Paul wanted to gain custody of our children and that he had acquired a lawyer to do so. I could barely pay the bills in our home, how was I going to afford a lawyer to fight for my children? They were so young; I could not allow that to happen. I talked to a few people and wound up getting a referral to an attorney that worked locally in our county who was willing to work with me. This was great news, but where would I get the money? From time to time, Paul would come by and buy flowers and try to make things work. It would feel good and it gave me hope. I was seeing glimpses of the man that I knew in the beginning, but I knew him well enough to know that this was nothing more than a temporary high. It was only to suck me back in, and I knew things would not change. I wasn't giving in and I believe that was making Paul upset. He would not cooperate with anything I suggested. There was no reason that we could not be cordial with each other. He refused to help pay the bills. Fine. If he didn't want to help with the bills, and he could no longer living in the house, then there was no point in me living there either. I couldn't afford it anyway. I set up an appointment with a realtor so that we could get the process started on selling the house. He showed up but all the things she instructed us to do, again, he refused. I was fed up with his antics. This made me know that I made the right decision in not getting back with him. I could not for the life of me understand why he was acting this way. I kept harping on the times he told me that if we were to split, we could always be friends and be cordial with one another. Then, I remembered that he rarely practiced what he preached. I became very frustrated. I had my phone in my hand and googled, "What to do when your husband is being difficult." I know that sounds weird, but I felt helpless. To my surprise the first thing that popped up was, *Narcissistic Personality Disorder*. It was a term that I'd never heard of. When I read the article, I was more than shocked, I was astounded! The characteristics described Paul in absolute detail. It was almost as if I were reading a story that was written exclusively about him. I started to do a lot of research on the subject and things became more evident that this is exactly what I was dealing with. My husband, ex-husband, separated partner, baby daddy—whatever he was at the moment—was a complete narcissist, and my life with him all began to make sense.

I didn't have much time to dwell on my findings. I had to take care of everything in the household and meet with my lawyer in the process of my divorce. I was blessed to have her. She gave me a plethora of information, in regard to what I was going through, and offered tremendous support. We had an unsuccessful mediation. Paul would not agree to the terms in which my lawyer and his, had mapped out. The final day in court was underway. I can't say that I wasn't nervous. Is this what I really wanted? This was a whole new chapter in my life. I couldn't believe that the marriage I worked so hard on, after so many years, was coming to an end. Even though I knew it wouldn't work, I was extremely sad. My lawyer was already there and welcomed me with a hug when I saw her. She asked if I was ready. As I nodded with uncertainty, we entered into the courtroom and greeted the judge. I looked around expecting to see Paul and his lawyer, but I never did. He never showed up. I could not understand why someone would cause so much uproar, make so many demands, and even request custody of his children, and NOT show up to the final hearing. Maybe Paul wanted to recant once again and thought that if he didn't show up things wouldn't go through. That was not the case. My lawyer was what you would call a 'savage,' and she made sure that the divorce was processed with or without Paul being in attendance. I didn't even know that could happen. When I got home that day, I felt numb. I didn't know how to feel. I didn't have any more tears left to cry. I was now a divorced woman, something I never wanted to be. One thing I can be absolute sure of was that I gave my heart into this marriage. I did not let go until I exhausted every possible solution to keep my marriage alive. So, because of that, I felt at peace. It didn't change the fact that major life changes were about to occur, but it did bring peace of mind. There was major healing that I needed to do and now I can do it. In the divorce decree, Paul was awarded the house. I didn't fight for it. I didn't want it. For what? After much thought, I decided that staying in that home would not be wise considering my in-laws and now ex-husband lived next door.

8

THE GREAT ESCAPE

I wish could tell you how brave I was. I wish I could tell you that I finally mustered up the nerve to leave on my own, but the truth is this, Paul filed for divorce. Even in freedom, he had a say in it. How pathetic is that? I didn't want to do it. However, this time, I was glad that he did. I may have not been strong enough to initiate, but I was certainly strong enough to oblige. The truth is, God made a way out for me. I think He knew how determined I was to make it work and He knew that it wouldn't do it on my own accord. I was ending a thirteen-year marriage and despite of what I thought I would feel, I was relieved. I contacted a realtor and began looking for my new humble abode. Although I was looking forward to new life, my old life was still clinging on. Paul was still being very difficult and trying to make this as hard as possible for me. Despite my wishes for him to stay out of the home until I moved, he continued to come over whenever I left and go through my things. From time-to-time he would even attempt to come over and act like we were a happily married couple. He called the police when I wanted to make proper arrangements for the kids. With everything that was going on, I wanted to give the kids as much normalcy and routine as I possibly could. It was one of the ways I was trying to shield them from our divorce. Paul had also started to talk negatively, about me, to our children. To make matters worse, despite the court orders, Paul was not voluntarily paying what he had agreed to. Not only were the bills not getting paid, at this point, I wasn't sure if I had enough money to move into a new place. I didn't have much time to worry about it. I HAD to make it happen. There were days where I didn't know whether I was coming or going. I was just going with the motions, trying to survive, and trying to provide for my children. I had to continue working and getting overtime, when I could, to maintain and get extra cash for the move. I also still had to be a mom. So, by this time, I was fed up, and the house hunting began. I had no clue where to start. To be honest, I'd never lived alone, and I've never looked for a home alone. I went from my mother's house to a married woman. I won't deny that I was scared. I most definitely was. However, I was still excited to find out what life had to offer outside of this chaotic world that I've lived in the past thirteen years. Paul was adamant on giving me the hardest time possible. Whenever the kids did go next door, they would always return with a distorted negative undertone. They would tell me inappropriate things that their dad would tell them about me. This was really difficult because I did not want to keep the kids from their dad, but I didn't want him to taint them either. I wasn't sure if this was his way to get under my skin, or if this was his grieving process. Either way, it needed to stop, immediately. I didn't want the kids involved in our affairs. His arrogance reared its ugly head again. One of my sons told me that his father inquired about our moving progress. He wanted to know if we had found an apartment yet. Insinuating that I couldn't afford a home on my own. The divorce was unpleasant enough, I didn't want us to be ugly toward each other, especially sending messages through the children. Apparently, he didn't care. I couldn't wait to get away from his grasp.

It was finally moving day, and the truck pulled up to the house. It was a bittersweet moment. I was torn because I was leaving the house that we had built from the ground up. The house that we had designed. The house in which we raised our children. The house that I was proud of and that we worked so hard for but, there was no Love on this Lane. For the sake of peace, I was also leaving the house of never-ending arguments. The house of constant confusion. The house that was a revolving door, with no boundaries. Yes, I was sad, but I was at peace. I was so glad to be away from the constant drama and secrets. I was ready to leave all of the confusion and secrets and chaos that came from next door. The place where all the traffic came in through the vehicle of judgement, overstepped boundaries, and disrespect. I can't tell you that my in-laws were not a help to me, because they were always there for the children, but it came with a cost. It was an exchange for my identity, familial background, and privacy. What I learned with Paul, and about narcissistic people was this: they will completely disregard all the years of loyalty, dedication, and companionship that you both shared. As I stated before, non-toxic people remember the good times even through the divorce, but you don't throw away all the good memories. In the narcissist's eyes, those times never existed. You are disposable. I shortly found out, after the divorce was final, that Paul had gotten married immediately following the divorce.

9

CO-PARENTING WITH A NARCISSIST

For a short time, I felt much needed peace that I hadn't had for a very long time. That would be short lived with Paul in the picture. Once he was given the address, he would pop up whenever he wanted, despite the court orders. I tried tirelessly to reason with Paul—to get him to follow the divorce decree—but he wouldn't. He acted like no one could tell him what to do, even a judge. He was above the law. In a way, he felt untouchable. It had gotten so bad, that Paul would come to my home, and pick up the children without asking me. He would even go to their schools, pick them up, and never mention a word to me. Technically, he needed consent on the days that were not his, to do this. Did Paul care? Nope! I would come home, in a panic, not knowing where my children were. If I called him, he would ignore the calls. The days that the children were in his possession, they would always return home upset and indifferent. I told myself that I wouldn't interrogate the kids when they came home from their dads, but I needed to know why they were acting this way. It seemed as if my ex-husband was trying to turn my own children against me. When I asked my youngest son, he would tell me all the negative things his dad would say about me. Not only was it wrong, it was incongruous for him to talk to the children about their mother. It was often that when the kids asked Paul for money for lunch or a school fee, he would tell them no and to ask your mom. Paul was constantly telling the children that I was taking all of his money and that I was being mean to him. Naturally, my kids thought I was the bad guy in all of this. As if a divorce wasn't enough to handle for a child, Paul was burdening his children with these conversations that were too heavy for their precious minds. I tried, on many occasions, to communicate with Paul through text messages, emails, and verbally to ask him to stop speaking with the children about adult affairs. My words just fell on deaf ears. As always, he did what he pleased, and completely ignored my wishes. It was just like our marriage—divorce was no different. It was impossible to co-parent with such a person. I always thought that if not anything else, we could reason for the sake of the children. Boy was I wrong. I soon realized that he, like all toxic parents, view children as tools and weapons to manipulate. One day, I was at work and received a phone call from the elementary school where my two youngest boys attended. It was the school counselor who began to tell me that the boys were in her office crying and upset. She told me that she noticed the boys crying when their dad dropped them off from his visit. She said that they were upset because their dad packed up everything that they owned at his house and put it all in black trash bags and dropped it off at my home and told them, " I'm sorry, I won't be able to see you guys anymore because your mom won't let me." I was devastated. I was so hurt for them. I spoke to them over the phone to calm them down and assured them that what their father told them was untrue. I tried to ease their minds so that they could have a good say at school, but deep down, I was livid! What kind of monster would play games with their children, and then send them to school upset? Was it to get to me, was it to make a point? Whichever it was, it was cruel. Every time I attempted to speak with him about issues regarding the children, he would start the circular, long, drawn out conversations again about something that happened years before. It was like driving into a dead end every time. My tactic in these instances was to contact his mother. I felt that maybe she could reason with him better than I could. I also thought maybe she would take into consideration the children's best interest, since he hadn't. I thought for sure moving away and getting a divorce would end the drama and turmoil, but it seemed that Paul would only crank it up a notch, or two. Children are mere pawns in his game of manipulation.

I thought leaving the marriage and the house next door would give me solitude. I thought it was the end to the emotional rollercoaster and theatrics. I quickly learned that it was only the beginning. There were many instances like this. Paul continued playing mind games with the children and when he didn't get his way, he would call the police on me. At times I had to call the police on him for taking the children outside of the designated dates, to get him to comply with the court orders. Many times, while I was at work, he would pick them up from school on my scheduled days and take them to his house. He did this purposely to get a rise out of me. Every time I called the police, things didn't work out in my favor. The police did not make him turn them over to me. It seemed as if he had friends on the police force. They seemed to favor him. They were rude to me and nice to him. You may think, why didn't I take him back to court to show that he was contempt of orders? To answer that question, it wasn't that easy. Going back to court required more money of which I didn't have. Paul's charm and manipulative nature was even rubbing off onto the police. Paul was enjoying the constant back and forth. I, on the other hand, was growing weary of it, and I was very concerned about my children's mental health. At times, it seemed that Paul's wicked plot to turn my own children against me was working. I couldn't get them to talk to me about their feelings. The times that I would have to fight to get them back home, after he stole them on my days, the children would ask me to let them stay—with him. That broke my heart but something in me had to continue to fight. I would not allow him to bully me. I would not allow him to control my home. Mostly, I would not allow him to corrupt my children. I began to pray like never before. The unwarranted visits continued, and since Paul payed for their phone bill, he thought he could just call them up and tell them to come outside as he pleased. When he did that, I started to take away their outside privileges—especially on my days. That was hard for me because I did not want to keep them from their dad. I also didn't want everything he was telling them to be valid which was "your mom is trying to keep you away from me." Instead, this was a way that I could maintain control in my home. Paul didn't like that I found a way to stop his controlling, bullying behavior. He even began telling people that I was keeping his children from him. I didn't care, I was enjoying the boundary that I had set because something was finally working. Well, it was working temporarily.

Paul was not letting up. I was convinced that his aspiration in life was to make mine a living hell. It was always one thing after the other. Every time the children would come home from their time with him, I had to do a detox on their thought process. He even talked negatively about their older brother and sister, Jaslyn and Zach. I had to be very intentional, all while not bashing him like he was doing me. This was not an easy task, and I didn't always triumph. I was angry that he would be mentally abusing his own children. I wanted them to know what he was doing, but I had to remember that their minds could not process what I wanted them to know. When I did try to get them to understand the mind games he was playing, it only backfired because they would say, "mom he says the same thing about you." I soon realized the best thing for me to do was to not say anything, and just be their mother. I learned that when in front of outsiders, Paul was good at performing like the super-parent. Unfortunately, it's the outsider's admiration that Paul is always after, not the children.

In all of the drama that I experienced I realized that narcissists don't co-parent, they counter- parent. They really don't care about the emotional and mental damage they are doing to their children as long as it hurts you. Unfortunately, children of toxic parents are also a source of supply to the narcissist. Sharing custody with a narcissistic parent is a daunting experience. They constantly undermine you and spit venom about you to your children. In my case, it's not a co-parent situation, it's mostly a compete-parent situation. There is very rarely any discipline or structure on his side. Paul's major goal was, and is, to outbuy me. He overindulged in buying gifts, giving money and taking the children on expensive vacations that I couldn't initially afford when we became a single-parent household. I was making sure that my children and I had the basic necessities. Paul, on the other hand, was living with his parents that yielded multiple incomes. He was comfortable and was able to splurge. He used that luxury to make sure that the kids knew that his house was the 'fun' house. He did it also in hopes that the children would choose to live with him. I stuck to my guns on this one and continued with structure and discipline as needed. Then eventually I was able to do the fun stuff. I refused to buy my children. They were not for sale, nor were they a bargaining ship. I was determined to earn their love and respect, and let God handle the rest.

10

REVISITING MY DISCOVERY

With no resolve, I continued to pray again, and something told me to go back and revisit the information I had read about narcissism. When I first stumbled upon the discovery of this term, I was living in my old house, still married, but separated from my ex-husband. Though I knew that discovery was true to my situation, I couldn't dig deeper, due to the fog that surrounded my existence at the time. Now that I was away, I had time and clarity of mind to dive into it. I was perplexed at Paul's behavior and why he was acting the way that he did. I had never seen anything like it before. I couldn't understand why, after being apart for so long, that he would not try to be peaceful with me for the sake of our children. I was shortly reminded when I began to take another look at the disorder. I studied, researched, and read books on the matter. I even watched videos for hours at a time, uncovering so many truths about what I had gone through and was still going through. My discovery gave me so much peace. I initially thought that I was the only one going through this type of relationship. The research showed that I was not. There are many other women, and men, dealing with relationships where their partner suffers from this personality flaw. As you read this, you may have thought that you were the only one as well. I am happy to say, there is a community of us out there, and we do not have to suffer in silence. When I started reading about this disorder, it was as if I was reading the story of my life. Everything that I had experienced in all of those years, with Paul and his family, all laid out, in detail, online. The revelation blew my mind to say the least. *Narcissistic Personality Disorder*, NPD, is characterized as a cluster B personality disorder in which a person has grandiose fantasies of success and power with little to no achievements.[1] People affected constantly compare themselves to others and have a strong sense of jealousy and envy that they are able to hide very well. In fact,

---

[1] American Psychiatric Association. (2013). *Diagnostic and statistical manual of mental disorders* (5th ed.). Washington, DC: Author.

they will act as if others are envious of them. They believe they are unique and special. They carry a sense of entitlement. They crave an insatiable amount of attention and admiration. In addition, they lack emotional empathy and have a willingness to exploit others for their own agendas. If you are reading this and it's describing your relationship in detail, I have good news and bad news. The bad news first. You are in a relationship with a narcissist and chances are it's toxic. The good news is, you've finally discovered the problem that you always knew was there but was unable to pinpoint the origin. There are so many different layers to this personality type. The tricky part is, you may think how can someone so charismatic, loving and giving be a narcissist? I was relieved to finally connect the dots. Behind this mask of extreme confidence, arrogant, and haughty attitude, was where Paul's true identity was hidden. That was the person that they didn't want anyone to see. People with NPD are master manipulators. That explained everything! It explained why I felt as if everyone around us was falling for the façade. Paul was a chameleon. He was one person at home, then an absolutely different person toward our mutual friends and family. He was whoever he needed to be, around whoever we were around at the moment. He was a social opportunist. He would cover up his flaws and offer me up to his family as the bad guy. Whenever I would bring it up, Paul always insinuated that I was crazy and imagining it. That's called gaslighting. *Gaslighting* is a manipulative tactic that narcissists use to sow seeds of doubt in your mind about something you may know to be true.[2] They make you question your own reality, memory, perception, and sanity. This tool is very effective because it's done slowly, and over a period of time, so you don't realize that it's happening. Next thing you know, you're brainwashed, and your perception of reality is really their perception ingrained within you. People with NPD are very strategic in doing this so that you would never know that it is happening. There are a few ways to tell if you are being gaslighted:

1). Outright lies. You may know that they are lying but they will lie with a straight face to throw you off your game. Next thing you know, you are questioning your belief, or you forget what the argument was even about.

2). Their actions do not match their words.

3). They deny that they ever said something, even though you know they did. That for sure will make you question your reality, because they are so convincing that you start to doubt yourself. Don't second guess yourself. Stand firm, or you will always fall to their feet.

4). They include positive reinforcement. They will alternate tearing you down with praising you for something you did. This

[2] Sarkis, S. (2018). Gaslighting: Recognize Manipulative and Emotionally Abusive People - and Break Free. New York: Da Capo.

keeps you engaged and prevents you from leaving when things get tough. They know that confusion weakens people's stability and normalcy.

5). They project their issues onto you. They are constantly accusing you of something that they are doing.

6). They tell other people that you are crazy. They know that once they've created a storyline against you, people will not believe you when things crumble.

There was a time that I caught Paul in a lie. I even had evidence, but he didn't know that I did. Of course, he denied it. Not only did he deny it, but he jumped up and down, and even cried. When I presented him with evidence that he couldn't refute, he just kind of looked stuck. Then he started to flip things around on me. I'm sure you're all too familiar with that scheme.

Narcissists hate authority. They are power hungry and see themselves as superior to others. They operate with a God complex and draw their strength from controlling other people. They want to be worshipped. You exist in their lives only to suit them. They are easily offended and highly sensitive to criticism. Do not question their authority. They expect you to be blindly loyal. They despise you if you don't measure up to their unrealistic expectations that they have set for you. They are usually very intelligent and ambitious. They work hard and appear to be overachievers, but they do this only to criticize others that have not aimed as high. They initially seduce you with flattery and are very lustful. If you have not come to the conclusion yet, this person hates you secretly. They have an agenda to destroy you. They have a natural flow where there is confusion and chaos. If confusion is not there, they will create it, hence all of the drama I endured. They will cause drama and then say that you are full of drama and they hate it. No matter how hard you try, nothing pleases them. You are in a no-win situation. You must get out.

11

WHERE DID IT START?

Narcissistic Personality Disorder is complex. A lot of people think that this just means that someone is into themselves and looking into the mirror all the time. People associate NPD as being self-centered and arrogant. Although this is true, NPD is so much more. Taking a look from a biblical standpoint, NPD sounds much like what's called the Jezebel spirit which can be found in 1st & 2nd Kings. They are known to twist the truth.

Narcissists appear confident and outgoing, but they are really insecure. They go to great lengths to mask their emotional vulnerability and insecurity. They present themselves as gentle and humble, even vulnerable and wounded at times. They also mirror traits of appearing concerned, compassionate, and helpful. However, they are extremely manipulative in using guilt and fear, covered in kindness, to bully people into getting what they want. You may notice that they portray themselves as committed to something bigger than themselves such as religion, education, enlightenment, or something of the sort. The absence of overt arrogance derails your suspicions. They give an illusion of being thoughtful and unselfish. They are indeed a wolf in sheep's clothing. If this person was immediately disrespectful, surely a self-assured person would not tolerate it. This kind is the most dangerous, because they are the trickiest to discern. They slowly break your confidence. They are very calculated in their technique. They find subtle ways to make you feel unimportant. Gradually over time, after they've nick-picked at your confidence and self-esteem, you'll start to feel diminished and you'll be left not knowing why. You won't know why because those subtle insults and put downs were presented as "jokes," and mixed with compliments and kind words to keep you engaged. Yet, you still are subconsciously thinking about the insults that were implanted in your mind. There were times that Paul took slights at my family, but never outwardly. He insinuated that he rescued me from my dark, dangerous, no end, background and gave me a better life. That was the disguise that he displayed. Hell, he even outwardly said it to me before. I had to remind Paul that though I came from an impoverished background and dysfunctional family, it was me that decided to go after a better life. It was plain to see that Paul thought that he was better than me and he expected me to be grateful for "resurrecting" my life. He acted as if I wasn't in school, striving for a better life, when he met me. I wasn't a housewife, with no degree, that totally depended on him to take care of me. We went to the same school, for the same degree, and worked nearly for the same pay—most of the time. I always worked and contributed half to all of the bills in the household, if not more. So, I'm not sure where Paul was getting this fairytale storyline from, but I was never a damsel in distress. He fed these lies to anyone that would listen. A narcissists persuasive behavior can be so cunning to the outsider, that they will undermine you with your own family, smear your name, and steal your money all while looking like a sincere, generous, upstanding citizen. Don't fall victim to their antics. When your Spidey senses or intuitions start to flare up, take that as a sign. Our gut knows—it always does.

WILLONA JEAN-PIERRE

12

LET THE SMEARING BEGIN

In an earlier chapter, I talked about the ways in which Paul would talk negatively about me to his family and friends. I believe that he had always done this, but I think that the slander increased as our marriage dissolved. Paul had an image to maintain, and by no means was I, or anyone else, going to get in the way of that goal. Paul knew that I had uncovered his true self, and he could not risk being exposed to the world. He wanted to make sure that people would take my words as a grain of salt. He basically silenced me before I could even open my mouth to speak. So, he started a smear campaign against me. This is a very common tactic that narcissists use. They do this in an effort to damage or call into question your reputation, credibility, and character by spewing out any negative information that they could find. It is very intentional and premeditated. They want to vilify you. Paul had done a lot of wrong to me, some things not even mentioned in this book, but I had no desire to shout it to the mountain tops. I had no desire to bad mouth him or make him look bad. I definitely had the power to, but I was exhausted of the whole ordeal, and I just wanted to move on with my life. I assumed he wanted the same. I was wrong. I was always wrong when trying to calculate his next move. I was perplexed until I discovered this information.

A smear campaign is character assassination in the form of rumors, half-truths, and lies. I couldn't believe some of the things that I heard him say about me to our family, friends, and children. Even when the facts behind a smear campaign lack proper foundation, the tactic is usually effective because the target's reputation is stained before the truth is known. This perfectly explains why he sent the damaging emails about me. He continued to smear my name. Even worse, he started to take the role of the victim. Narcissists have been bold enough to contact your relatives to talk about you. I found out years later that Paul had contacted various family members of mine, or anyone who would listen, to spew blatant lies about me. They will go to great lengths to trash your name and put you at fault, in order to lead others to believe that you are crazy. If you're dealing with a narcissist, it's inevitable that this has happened to you. The ex-partner that they will use as the scapegoat will also be the same person they are trying to destroy. Fight the desire to want to defend yourself and exonerate yourself from the lies. There's a scripture in the Bible, in the book of Proverbs 26:4 that says, "Do not answer a fool according to his folly or you will be just like him." People will come to realize that the "crazy ex," who's described by the narcissist as psycho, is really the victim, and the narcissist is the abuser. The people that know you, will automatically know the truth, and that's all that matters. Eventually the truth will come to light. It did for me.

WILLONA JEAN-PIERRE

13

THAT'S ABUSE!

After the smoke cleared from the divorce, I was left to deal with everything that I had encountered over the last 15 years. With all of the new information that I had uncovered about who Paul really was, the type of relationship that I was involved in, and everything in between, I was finally ready to start a new chapter in my life and heal. But, heal from what exactly? Healing from something indicates that there has been a wound somewhere. There were definitely wounds. I'd come to the discovery that I had been abused. Some may wonder how I was abused. You didn't have any black eyes, or bruised ribs. You never were hospitalized for broken bones. Hell, I don't even think I can recall a scratch on me to be honest. So, how was I abused? Most people learn to identify signs of physical abuse but, in these instances, the abuse is not so obvious. You won't believe or understand that you were in an abusive relationship until long after it's over because there weren't physical scars to represent the abuse. You won't truly be able to move on unless you acknowledge the fact that abuse has occurred. After escaping a relationship with a narcissist, you may feel completely drained and exhausted because you were in a constant state of fight or flight for so long. You've been told that you were crazy for so long, that you started to believe it. However, when you remove yourself from this toxic environment, and the fog begins to clear, you feel relief, but you also see the lasting effects of that relationship. That is abuse. You are no longer the outgoing, bubbly, confident person you were before this relationship started. What happened to you was intentional. It was a ploy to destroy you. The narcissist hated everything about you that they couldn't embody. Every positive characteristic in you was targeted because they despised the fact that they couldn't exhibit them, so the plan was to chip away at the core of who you were in order to control you. Emotional abuse is an attempt to control through manipulative tactics that, in the end, causes psychological trauma. Emotional abuse is elusive. Any form of abuse is horrible, but emotional abuse goes unnoticed because both parties, on the giving and receiving end, may not even realize it's actual even occurring.

When people hear the word abuse, they are used to seeing evidence of marks, scars and bruises. Emotional abuse causes internal scars that people cannot see, and it is immensely ignored, but just as powerful. It can be more harmful than physical abuse because it can undermine what we think about ourselves. Physical abuse can harm your body and even result in murder. A narcissist using emotional abuse can kill your soul and spirit. Below, a list of indicators are presented to show the different ways that emotional abuse can be presented:

1. Telling you how you should feel or act
2. Isolating you from family and/or friends
3. Constant threats of leaving
4. Shows complete disregard and disrespect to your opinions and ideas
5. You have to walk on eggshells when they are around
6. You feel like you're not free to discuss problems without them getting upset and turning things around on you
7. You feel stuck and confused
8. You feel that nothing you say or do is good enough
9. They belittle you in front of people—may be direct or subtle
10. They play mind games/accuses you of being crazy

Emotional abuse has been very hard to define. It has been said that, emotional abuse is experienced more than recognized. Most times, only after you experience it can you recognize it.

14

HE DROPPED A BOMB ON ME

If you have come out of a relationship with a narcissist, or are still in one, you may find yourself trying to return your relationship to the days where the love was new, the feeling was right, and life was simple. You work hard to 'fix' something that, you didn't break, only to find things are one sided and, all on you. You are putting your all into the relationship, but the other person isn't. Essentially, you are in a relationship, alone. You may think if you work hard enough you can fix it. If you do enough, things will go back to the way they used to be. In the beginning you went through what's called the 'Love Bomb' phase. Let's take a trip back down memory lane.

You remember how they treated you. It was as if the world revolved around you and you were on cloud nine. Ok, now think a little harder, a little deeper. Do you remember how amazing it was when you realized that you both had everything in common? Paul and I liked all of the same things, movies, music, and food. You had the same political views, same goals, and even liked to travel. I mean, it was uncanny. You even shared the same family values. You finally met someone that is interested in all the same things as you. You felt like you had finally hit the jackpot. Cha-ching! You thought, finally, my soulmate! It feels good to be loved adored and appreciated by someone. Love Bombing, also known as the idealization phase, is a tool used by a highly manipulative narcissist to seduce their prey. They mirror you and learn things that you like and deliver them on a silver platter. They excessively praise you with flattery, gifts, compliments and even profess their love for you early on. They are gentlemen, opening doors, and even take you out on expensive vacations or extravagant dates. They take their time with you. It seems intoxicating, and that's because it is. Love feels good and you want that feeling to continue. I mean let's be honest, you deserve to be happy! Why not now? Why not this moment? Only this is not true love, you're being groomed without your awareness or consent. You engage because you've been promised a loving secure future. Sex is explosive and the connection is undeniable. They place you on a pedestal. In the process we become invested and the bond becomes stronger than ever. It is on another level physically, emotionally, and spiritually. We feel the need to live up to the image of perfection that they have placed upon us. They make us believe that we are the center of their world. In turn, we labor to remain so in their eyes, and we place them in the center of ours. That's where things get hazardous. In the love bombing phase, the narcissist is getting you to put your guard down and open up about things you normally wouldn't. It's slow and subtle. They get you to trust them and depend on them as someone you can turn to. You become vulnerable. You become accessible to their manipulation. Over a period of time, when I wasn't paying attention, that's when I gave Paul power over me. It doesn't feel like it, but this is where the abuse starts. The person that the narcissist is presenting to you in this stage is not real. It's a mask they put on to get you to expose yourself to them. They can also escape their own emptiness by using our loving hearts as a safehouse. We empty out our heart to pour it out to them in abundance, only to be sucked dry. By the time you realize it, much like me, you'll be well into the relationship, hooked. You will never see it coming. Yet, you will feel yourself slipping away. The moment you start to lose your identity, is the moment they have invaded the very essence of who you are. That is what they want. That is how they win.

15

DON'T MAKE ME GET THE FLYING MONKEYS

I'm sure you've seen, or have heard, of the movie the *Wizard of Oz*. There is a scene where the Wicked Witch of the East sends out her flying monkeys to do her bidding, upon her command, and attack people on her behalf. This is a visual illustration of the work of a narcissist. The narcissist has a fan club of people that he/she has recruited to be on their side against the victim in smear campaigns. These people are usually friends or loved ones. Narcissist use family members to maintain their illusion of power over you. Narcissist employ the use of third parties in an attempt to continue to control and manipulate you. The narcissist wants to attack you publicly and make you appear to be the bad guy. They have to be seen as the good person.

Privately they have hand selected people to complain to, about you, and whom would feel sorry for them. They are, essentially, building their support system. You are now being portrayed as the evil one, and they need protection from you. After this information has been carefully injected into the person, they are instructed to attack you, in order to keep him safe. They choose people who will make an easy target. Narcissists collect people who make them feel important. They aren't only manipulating the person that they are in a romantic relationship with, but also those around them. So, at this point, we are all his prey. The only difference is, his "support system" are his minions, and you are the target. They use them for supplies, for means, and for an exit. This is not a friendship, it's parasitic. They also know who won't participate in their game, so they avoid those people. The narcissist slowly poisons the mind of his minions until they and fueled with the same hate that he has. They make these stories so believable and emotionally intense that the flying monkey becomes enraged at you, on the narcissist's behalf. They become upset that you, or anyone else, could hurt their precious son, friend, brother, father, etc. They are completely sold on the idea that the narcissist is the good guy. The flying monkey will spread lies repeated to them. They do this believing they are supporting an innocent person. The lie doesn't come directly from the narcissist. They have his minions do his bidding so that, at the end of the day, his hands are clean. These people have no idea they are being used. The narcissist continues to encourage this, and the flying monkey is rewarded with the idea that they are protecting the narcissist or doing what is right. Another reason that a narcissist continues to keep flying monkeys (or minions) around is because they don't like to be alone. That explains why there were always people around. They don't want to be left alone with themselves. They're boring, uninteresting, monotonous, and empty and they know it. They need excitement from others. They need insight on how to act and how to exist in the world from others. Family members don't typically have malicious intent. They are completely misled. Remember that narcissists are manipulative and charismatic. They are very convincing, cunning, ad divisive. That makes it hard for most people to see through them. If you have no experience with this type of person, then you wouldn't be able to see the signs. If you're a genuinely good person, you don't think that anyone has a reason to lie and manipulate, so you believe them because who would blatantly construct such lies? That is what makes narcissists so dangerous. They feed off the innocent, the pure, the good, and use it to their advantage. It's crazy to think that these people really do exist. You may be thinking what the best way is to deal with a family member situation. Should you try to convince them you are right? The best thing to do in this instance is to do exactly what I did, NOTHING! You deal with them just as you do with the narcissist—no contact at all. They won't believe you anyway. It's pointless. They will eventually find out on their own. It will take time just as it did you. Narcissists can only keep up their act for so long. Their whole existence is built on lies. Eventually, things will start to become clearer to the flying monkey when the narcissist's lies start to not add up anymore. But, at the end of the day, it will be their choice to stick around once they discover the truth. Steer clear of both parties and don't attempt to engage to clear your name. As the saying goes—Not my circus, not my monkeys.

16

WHY DID HE CHOSE ME?

People have a misconception that narcissists choose weak, easily influenced people. That may be true for some. In other cases, the narcissist chose you for the exact opposite reason. You were carefully selected because of your strength, success, intelligence, and independence. You have many more resources to offer and you make a great trophy for their image. Empaths are what narcissists are not, empathetic. Empaths are prone to want to fix others. Co-dependency is a dysfunctional helping relationship where one person supports and enables another person's addiction, poor mental health, immaturity, irresponsibility, or underachievement. Some refer to it as relationship addiction. An empath tends to focus on others at their own expense.

The relationship is usually one sided, where the toxic person relies on the other for all of their emotional and self-esteem needs. Almost like a one stop shop. If you've ever flown on an airplane, you know that before the plane takes off the flight attendant gives safety instructions. They tell you that in case of an emergency, the oxygen masks will drop down before you assist someone else, make sure that you have properly placed your own oxygen mask first. The reason for that is simple. You cannot help anyone else if you are not alive. You are not able to save another life, unless your life is first secured and stable from danger. Both the co-dependent and the narcissist are unhealthy. Co-dependents lack self-esteem and have unhealthy relationships with themselves. They tend to put others before themselves. Narcissists also have unhealthy relationships with themselves. The difference is, the narcissists put themselves and their needs before others. Co-dependents put others before themselves. It's very easy for these types of people to find each other. They're like a magnet. While the narcissist may come off as needing direction and guidance, because they play their role of victim so well, they really don't need you, they want what you have, or what they can gain from you. It's an unequal relationship where one side gives all and the other takes all. When the co-dependent doesn't see any change, they blame themselves into thinking that if they love them more, the narcissist would finally change, and they will get the partner that they desire. The co-dependent person doesn't realize that there isn't anything in the world that will be enough for their narcissistic companion. Narcissists are empty on the inside with a hole at the bottom. A deep, black, never ending hole. Nothing ever fills them. The co-dependent ends up pouring out everything they have and not having enough left for themselves, or anyone else. Co-dependents find themselves pushing aside their own dreams and aspirations for acceptance. This happens because their goals threaten the existence of the narcissist. Dreams make the narcissist feels small and insignificant. So, to accommodate for their feelings, you find yourself suppressing things you are passionate about. It forces you to become a watered-down alternate version of yourself. The narcissist is stripping you of your identity without your knowledge or consent. You, as the co-dependent, have become an enabler because you think you can fix the narcissist. Newsflash, you cannot fix the narcissist. You allow the narcissist to dump all of their emotional baggage onto you because you believe you can handle it. You're strong right? You're intelligent right? Something like this can't happen to you, right? Remember, they are very aware of your strengths, that's why they chose you. You cannot handle what you thought you could. Co-dependents confuse caretaking and self-sacrifice of their true identity with love and loyalty. That is not loyalty or love. That is character assassination.

WILLONA JEAN-PIERRE

17

WHY CAN'T I LEAVE?

Have you ever witnessed someone in an abusive relationship and wonder why won't they just leave? You wonder how they could have endured this mistreatment for so long, for so many years? You may be thinking of yourself in a relationship, and asking yourself, "Why can't you muster up the nerve or strength to leave? Why would someone put up with a significant other that treats them so cruel?" While there can be a few different answers to these questions, there's one in particular that is true for many: *Trauma Bond*. A trauma bond is loyalty or commitment to a person who is harmful and damaging to you. A traumatic bond can form rapidly and last long, even after the relationship is severed. A few conditions are necessary for this to occur; someone is threatened with danger, harsh treatment, alternated with small acts of kindness, isolation from others' perspective, and a belief that there is no escape.[3] When you think of the word bond, you may naturally think love. You may think of a significant other, or a friend, that you both have a strong bond with, in a positive manner. Truth is you can have a negative bond with someone as well. A great example of this is *Stockholm Syndrome*. Despite the initial threat of being held captive, the bond happens when the captor shows the hostages that they choose not to kill them. The captives are relieved at the initial threat of death and their feelings are then transferred to feelings of gratefulness to the captor for allowing them to stay alive. They convert small acts of kindness from the perpetrator as good treatment under the circumstances. Psychologist coined this phrase as a better way to understand the relationship between abusers and victims. The same concept happens in trauma bonding in toxic relationships.

You remember the cycle of abuse: Love bomb, devalue, and discard? In that process you are being groomed. In the love bombing phase things are foggy and you can't see past the high of love or through the smoke of affection. When you are in "love," in the beginning you won't notice the pattern.

---

[3] Vaknin, S., & Rangelovska, L. (2015). *Malignant self love: Narcissism revisited.* Skopje: Narcissus Publications.

If you don't notice the pattern you won't be able to recognize it, and you for sure won't be able to stop it. Hence if you don't see the cycle, you end up in a relationship, or marriage, for long periods of time, even years. Over a period of time, you begin to let your guard down and become more vulnerable. That's the point that you handed over your power. So, the cycle of abuse continues, next up devalue, discard. You end up trying harder and harder to satisfy them to no avail. It's hard to pinpoint the cycle because things are so foggy for you. After you get tired of going back and forth you try to leave but, the narcissist pulls you back in. They'll lie to get you to stay and tell you how things are going to change. You feel a super connection to the person, so you stay. This constant cycle is keeping you trapped. You're unaware but you are now addicted to this person. The human body has hormones. One in particular is *Dopamine*. In short, dopamine controls the reward and pleasure centers in the brain. It helps with reinforcement, where you do the same things over and over. It creates repetition. This is where habits are formed. It also controls emotional responses. Another hormone I will touch on is *Oxytocin*. This hormone has components that involve bonding and forming trust between people, while it reduces stress and anxiety. Basically, this drug makes you defenseless. And here we thought Oxytocin was just to induce labor in pregnancy. The constant abuse cycle that the narcissist has put you through has created a major imbalance of the chemicals causing extreme craving and yearning for your partner. The trauma bond is a result of the abuse cycle. Scientists compare this to heroin addiction because of the intensity of the craving. All you keep thinking about is the first hit of love bomb that you received in the beginning of the relationship, that you endure the abuse. You are so high off their love that you downplay the abuse, rationalize their behavior, and try to find their sweet spot again—by any means necessary. You end up only getting crumbs thrown at you. When your body releases these hormones, your mind gets accustomed to and now it's considered normal for you. You are addicted to the peace that comes afterward, so you accept it. You accept less and less, and now they can get away with more and more. He got you to lower your expectation for the relationship as opposed to the high hopes you had in the beginning. Your brain is naturally wired to keep you safe by remembering good times. In this situation however, that's not a good thing because it makes you forget or downplay the bad, hence allowing the abuse. Here are a few reasons why I didn't want to leave, and it may be true for you as well—give or take a few.

Firstly, I didn't want a failed marriage. Secondly, I stayed for the children. Thirdly, I didn't want my children to go through the emotional turmoil of divorce. Fourthly, I pondered on the good times in hopes that there would be more to come. Fifth, I thought if I was patient and prayed hard enough things would change. Last, but certainly not least, I didn't want to leave all that I had worked for.

The intensity of this bond explains why the break up is so hard. When you finally leave it feels like you are detoxing from a drug. The good news is, that intoxicating bondage can be broken with distance and prayer. We need to learn to discern good soul ties from bad ones. The best way to recognize the difference is to note that a connection to a good soul tie gives you power, an attachment to a negative soul tie sucks the life out of you.

WILLONA JEAN-PIERRE

18

HIGH ROAD TO HEALING

Even though I divorced my husband after thirteen years, and moved into another home, I still had a load of baggage to carry. The process of healing would be a long road, but I had to start. For many years after, I didn't even know that I had been abused. I did not understand the depth of what I had been through until I started to research the disorder and looked at the treatment I received in hindsight. The more knowledgeable you become about *Narcissistic Personality Disorder*, the easier it makes for healing. You will begin to understand and put things into perspective. It will begin to make sense. For me, the biggest part of my healing came from this revelation; A crucial part of healing started when I accepted the fact that I wasn't even in a real relationship. First, I had to grieve the person I thought my husband to be. I came to a realization that I was in love with a make-believe person in a make-believe marriage. Even though it was real to me, it was not to him. I was in love with a falsified identity that he displayed all those years. That, in itself was devastating, because you're mourning a fantasy. Secondly, I grieved the truth. The person that he really was, resided underneath the mask. The person who hurt me, lied to me, treated me with no regard, and used me for his own personal sick gain, was Paul. He never loved me at all. That too was devastating and an absolute truth that I had to face. I had to grieve twice, and it was twice as painful. The start of this process helped me to understand that healing is done in layers. There may be moments where you feel stupid for falling for such a person. I want to encourage you to lose this thought. You were groomed, lied to, and manipulated. This is NOT your fault! They have spent a lot of time learning their craft. You were unprepared. Breaking up with someone with this magnitude of toxicity is like recovering from a stroke. You have to re-learn some of the most basic things of your daily life. This is because, slowly and subtly, your identity was being eradicated. You may have felt that something is wrong with you that made the narcissist treat you so badly. I had a lot of hurt that I covered up well but needed to be dealt with. I wasted so much anger on this relationship. I had discovered information about Paul—in addition to things that I knew about him personally—his family, and his upbringing that could destroy him, if I wanted. Revenge would be sweet, but I didn't want revenge. I wanted to heal. The best revenge is no revenge. I realized that recovery from toxic relationships would be a lot more work than a traditional one. I definitely had lost myself. At least who I have known myself to be. I didn't know who I was anymore. Not in a sense where I didn't truly know myself, but in a sense where I dummied myself down to not overshadow him. I suppressed my passion as to not interfere with the agenda of the family. I think there's a high percentage of women that do this in family, and relationships, because we think it's a woman's sacrifice to her family. In fact, it is just the opposite. *Denying one's own purpose and passion is an injustice to who God created you to be.* We are to operate in the fullness of why we were created. Anything less than that causes us to walk in sadness and confusion. That is not life and life abundantly, as the Bible states.

Not only is your heart broken from the relationship, but someone tried to break you down, take your identity, and erase you for good. That is a betrayal that is difficult to recover from. When you finally break the stronghold that they had on you, you gain a whole new outlook on life. There is a liberation you get when rediscovering yourself again. It's almost like being released from prison. You get to do things you haven't been able to do for a while, without someone else's opinion being infringed upon you.

A key point to remember here is to not wait or want closure from a relationship like this. Majority of toxic situations will not get you closure, an explanation, or an apology. Don't let this hinder your healing process. You have to keep in mind that master manipulators like this, will not only give you a fake apology, but they are probably not going to give you one at all. They don't think they've done anything wrong. Don't blame yourself for what happened. Don't blame yourself for how long you stayed. Don't blame yourself for falling for their lies. You had no idea someone would fake a whole identity to destroy you. What is the likelihood of something like that happening?

You don't have to feel bad, or apologize, for the need to be alone. A lot of people that I have met along the way did not understand this. They didn't know my history. It was too much to explain. Never feel the need to explain it unless you are led. Solitude is part of your healing journey. Silence is needed in this time. You may need to cry, sleep, pray, or just ponder and reflect on what you have experienced. You need to sort things out—You and God alone. Let God replenish and restore what was lost in this season. You will start to remember who you are and whose you are. You will start to remember what your passions are and what makes the fire ignite inside of you. Your light was put out by the narcissist. It's time for the pilot light to be relit.

After some time, I woke up with a renewed sense of clarity. I started to feel strong again. Parts of me that were buried started to reemerge. What you have to do is unravel lies and replace them with truth. You have to remember you. You do this by learning what God says about you to refute the lies that he told you about yourself. Deprogramming from the abuse that you endured is vital so that you don't remain imprisoned to the voice of that toxic person that was in your mind. Practicing self-care helps you to set boundaries. Meditate on the word of God and let His voice silence the constant roaring voice of the enemy. An essential key is to also let go of the need to please people. That's what got you into this mess in the first place.

Becoming familiar with what you've experienced is important, but there's a more pivotal key to your healing. That key is forgiveness. Don't disregard the idea just yet. Some people believe they have a right to be mad at their abuser, especially with all the things that you've endured at their hand. I'm not here to refute that, as I understand the intensity of what you've experienced; you have every right to be angry. The problem is, you can be only be angry for so long. Anger turns into hate, then into bitterness. It's like the saying goes, "You drink poison in hopes that the other person drops dead." Prolonged anger only hurts you. It is not healthy to harbor resentment toward the person. Forgiveness will help you to move on with your life. Although you feel justified, you have no right to not forgive. Matthew 6:14-15 says, "For if you forgive other people when they sin against you, your heavenly father will also forgive you. But if you do not forgive others, your Father will not forgive you." It doesn't seem fair does it? But God does not think or work like we do. We have done things in our lives that require forgiveness as well. In order to be set free of those things, we have to be willing to extend grace as it has been shown to us. This may be one of the hardest things you have done, but you have to do it to move on. The pain and hurt you experienced is real and I can definitely empathize with it. I can equally assure you that living with unforgiveness will only hinder your life and destroy your own soul. Although you feel that you haven't done anything wrong, unforgiveness is a sin to God. Acts 3:19 says, "Times of refreshing will come when you repent." What you need more than ever is time of refreshing. Real healing can only come from God, from the inside out. Forgive again and again, until you feel the burden lifted. Forgiveness is a choice. It does not mean you have to rekindle the relationship; it just means you release them from your heart and soul. It may take time but continue to trust God. I challenge you to do things differently to gain different results. I noticed during my experience that talking to friends didn't always get me very far. In fact, it made me relive the moment and become angry all over again. Yes, I got to vent, and it made me feel good for the moment, but it kept me in the moment. Your friends most likely mean you well and may very well be trying to help. Unfortunately, they don't have the answers. Before telling anyone anything I recommend that you pray to God about it. When I did this, I received peace and wisdom on how to handle situations. It also helped me gain self-control. Times where I would have lashed out, I was able to think more rationally after prayer. This comes from a scripture that a good friend introduced me to long ago. It is now embedded in me. Philippians 4:6 says, "Do not be anxious about anything, but in every situation, by prayer and petition, with thanksgiving, present your requests to God." To me that means, don't worry about anything but pray about everything, tell God all about it and He will give you peace. I can attest that God has kept His promises in this scripture. Worry won't get us anywhere. It won't add another day to our lives. In fact, stress is one of the leading causes of death, and worry is the cousin to stress. It is better to seek and trust God in this hour like never before. Like my dad always said, "over time not overnight." You've got this!

MEET THE AUTHOR

Willona Jean-Pierre

Performing artist, mother of 5 and lover of life, Willona Jean-Pierre is a Chicago native and is on the move! In her first book, she chronicles her experience about the weight she carried to make it through a toxic relationship. Once voiceless by the hands of her narcissistic husband, now a trailblazer in advocating for individuals that share similar experiences. She is at her prime and will indeed make a huge impact on the world in the time to come. Willona Jean-Pierre, definitely a name you should know!

CONTACT AUTHOR

Want to schedule a book signing or speaking event, or submit confidential questions with the author?

Complete the contact form at
www.willonajean-pierre.com

Instagram@ WJPandCompany

WANT TO WRITE A BOOK?

Contact our publisher at
www.drnesintl.com

Made in the USA
Las Vegas, NV
25 September 2023